Teddy-Johnny *and me*

A Memoir of Australian Speedway

Geoffrey Grocott

ISBN-13 978-1501021473
ISBN-10 1501021478

Chalkylee Publishing

TO MY FATHER

FREDERICK FRANCIS GROCOTT D.C.M.

SYDNEY 1960

I often think of that long ago summer day. The three of us mucking around with motorbikes in front of the old house at Mascot. Mum and Rosemary are there.

We must have been all of eighteen. We thought we could fly. In a few short years, everything changed forever.

CONTENTS

1951 BOTANY

Minnie introduced me to motorcycles. Not that we ever exchanged so much as one word. I doubt he even knew I existed. I was just another kid hanging outside Bill's milk bar on the Botany Road. Botany big kids didn't talk to Botany little kids. It was a Sunday arvo, my best mate Billy Walters and I were sitting on the bench seat outside Bills. And bored stiff. We couldn't go swimming because it was winter, and we'd already been over to the Water Works to catch some pigeons. Billy said we should jump on a tram and go somewhere but we didn't have enough money. We thought about walking across the new road to have a look at the planes landing, but we'd done that last week. We just sat on that seat bored out of our brains.

A couple of kids were inside playing the pinball machine. We were about to join them when Minnie and his jet-black Triumph Thunderbird pulled up right in front of us. Minnie never wore a helmet. They were for sissies and Minnie was sure no sissy. Everyone in Botany knew Minnie, and everyone in Botany knew the coppers were after him. They had no chance; Minnie was the fastest man in town.

Minnie stopped the engine. pulled the Trumpy on its stand. and slowly unzipped his black leather jacket. He looked around then threw back his white silk scarf and dropped his leather gloves onto the Thunderbird's seat. Minnie walked into Bills and we followed. 'Double chocolate malted,' barked Minnie. The fastest man in Botany didn't do please. Bill plopped a heavy soda glass on the counter and was about to pour the chocolate malted when Minnie put his hand up. No soda glass for him, the fastest man in Botany took his shake straight from the steel container. Down it went. Minnie wiped his gob with the back of his hand and threw a couple of bob on the counter.

1

All done Minnie walked out and again we followed.

Minnie jumped back on the Thunderbird and with one kick roared off. Straight past the cop shop. Minnie didn't care, they would never catch him. From that moment, I knew I too would one day have a Triumph Thunderbird. And from that day on I took my milkshakes straight. Just like the fastest man in Botany.

A few months later I was in our lounge room. My dad was reading the afternoon paper. Something on the front page caught my eye. In bold letters, the headline announced, "**Sydney's number one traffic menace stopped.**" It was Minnie.

2

1952   SYDNEY SHOWGROUNDS

Keithy Warren was my best friend at Banksmeadow Public. Keithy had the world's best grandmother who made the world's best cakes, and lots of other good stuff. As Keithy lived next door to his grandmother, whenever possible I walked home with him. I had never even seen my grandmothers so I didn't know if they made great cakes and other good stuff. Granny Grocott had millions of other grand-kids, and Granny Newton was mad, or so my mother said. And as they both lived far away in the bush it was unlikely I'd ever get to see them. At times I secretly wished Keithy's granny was my granny, his family my family. I didn't know if Keithy's dad was in the war, but he sure was different to my dad. They were always doing things. Like playing soccer and going for long car rides, and going to the Showground Speedway every Saturday night. The Warrens were good at the soccer thing too. Later Johnny Warren, one of Keithy's cousins, captained Australia.

I didn't know much about this Speedway place the Warrens went to every summer Saturday night. Keithy said it was a big deal and heaps of people went there. One day Keithy's dad asked if I'd like to go with them. The next Saturday night I was at the Sydney Showgrounds with the Warrens. Keithy bought some hot chips from the Tassie potato van and we headed for the

Suttor stand. The same families went every week and Keithy's family seemed to know just about everyone around them. If anyone was a bit late, the others minded their place till they got there.

After a while a big noise came from under the stand across from us. Keithy said it was the bikes warming up and we went down to the fence to watch the first race. Keithy had some gas glasses he picked up from the track the week before. He said the riders bought them from Army disposal stores and always wore a few so they could throw away the top pair when they got dirty. They looked flimsy but Keithy reckoned all the riders used them and to put them on, otherwise we'd cop dirt in our eyes. I didn't know what he was talking about but I put them on anyway. All the while I was thinking, if these stupid things were all my dad wore over there, any wonder he coughed all the time.

Finally, the noise stopped and the Big Ben clock started to chime. Next thing the track lights came on and some motorbikes were wheeled out for the first race. They started their engines and one by one rode slowly towards the starting line tapes. Then suddenly the tapes flew high and all the lights except those on the track went out.

The riders flew towards the first corner and I learned why Keithy wanted me to wear those gas goggles. As the bikes flashed past they sprayed us with heavy wet dirt. Next lap they were back, and going so fast I was sure they wouldn't make the corner. But they did, and hit us with even more dirt. Two laps later it was over.

Then the sidecars came out. They were even crazier. The blokes on the side, Keithy called them the passengers, were scraping the track. I ran back to the stand to sit with the adults.

At last the meeting was over and thankfully no one was hurt. I had dirt all over my clothes, but at least the goggles had stopped any from getting in my eyes. On the way home, Keithy's dad asked if I wanted to come next week. I said I was going fishing or something, I sure never wanted to go back to that mad place.

3

2012   HALE STREET BOTANY

I come to Hale Street every now and then. Not very often, but I do at times. It was here my dreamy childhood ended the day my mum left. I remember the suitcase. The taxi waiting. My father's tears when he arrived home from work. He hadn't seen it coming. My father was a shearer, but his younger wife, my mother, wanted to be in the city. There he was a fish out of water and she left anyway. My father was knocked about in the First World War. Who knew what demons he carried inside?

Hale Street Botany is just another busy industrial estate. Trucks roar by. Planes fly low. Wall to wall factories. Few know it was once a quiet fishing village that fronted the bay, and the bay was good. Little trace of those days remain, though if you look close enough there are still a few signs.

There were only three streets to the village. Hale, Luland, and Booralee. Timber workmen's cottages with their front doors opening to the footpath. And kids, lots of kids.

We hadn't been here long when the first factory came. No resident action groups then, or maybe no one cared. Eventually the fishing was over and the fisher families left. After a while the beach gave way for a road to the new container port. No more wooden clinker fishing boats laying on their side at low tide. Nor fishing nets mended in the sun alongside the Fisherman's Club house. Everything trampled by the industrial machine.

It was the early fifties when we moved to Hale Street. Our third Sydney house since we left my father's hometown of Yass. This time we had only come from Hastings Street on the other side of Botany Road but Hale Street was another world. The fibro house was modern on maybe half an acre. At first the block was wild and overgrown. My father soon made it into a small farm. Chooks, veggies, pigeons and fishponds. A kid's paradise. My dad could build anything. I can't even cut a straight line.

Then she left and before long we left. A little later they put a big factory over our once farm. Many years later I returned to find the factory old and empty, though our house was still standing. Both derelict, windows smashed, rubbish strewn around. No sign of life. I didn't go in.

Once as I waited in line at a Tasmanian hardware shop, I glanced at the label on the can of paint I was about to buy. There it was in black and white. "Manufacturer's address, Hale Street, Botany" I was homesick and wanted to shout, 'Hey, I used to live there.' Then I thought of Dad. I put the paint back, I didn't need reminders.

2012 and the factory that replaced our little farm too has gone. Everything I remember covered in fresh concrete. The sign, "Factory Units for Sale."

My parents were outsiders in Fisherman's Village. They didn't drink, and my mother had a full-time job when most women stayed at home. Not that the fisher people were unfriendly. Far from it. But we were different. Mum and Dad never visited the fisher's clubhouse by the beach on a Sunday afternoon. Nor the pubs up on Botany road. Or the footy. My parents were happier at home, or so it seemed. I spent my time fishing and catching pigeons at the Botany Water Works. Hanging out with the fisher kids.

One day as I was cleaning the pigeon house my dad told me how his brother Frank went to a pigeon training course in the war. They sent him across the channel and my dad was happy cause it got his little brother away from the front line, for a while.

Dad marched every April with the medals pinned to his chest. One year I marched too, a drummer with the Botany Scouts. After Mum left, we never marched again.

4

1956 BOTANY

With Mum gone, things were quiet in the house on Hale Street. Sometimes I went to my friends though that upset me more as I was the only one without a mum. I didn't know where she was, and most of the time my father walked around in a daze. He still went to work every day, and our red kelpie still ran for the paper when Dad got off the tram. But everything else had changed. We ate dinner in silence then I'd retreat to my room. One day I went to Kings Cross and got a couple of dumb tattoos. I didn't know why. For a long time I managed to keep them secret. Any interest I had in high school was long gone, my marks dreadful. I began to think about dropping out. I didn't talk about it with Dad, he had enough problems.

One day, instead of school I walked into Australian Wool and Produce on the hill at Banksmeadow. After all the work my parents did in helping me gain a place in a selective high school, I just walked away. Not the smartest thing I've ever done.

At fourteen, I was a sort of a packer stuffing wool into big hessian bales, as Botany boys did. It was hard hot work, but better than school because I got paid at the end of the week. My father was not one bit happy when he found out. After a few arguments he dropped the subject and we returned to silence. Later they offered me a cadetship for a wool classer, or something like that. Dad would have been pleased. But of course, I didn't take up their offer, all too sensible for me. One day I simply walked away from the wool place, again I didn't know why.

The only person I cared about was my girlfriend. Everyone said Pam was the best sort in Botany, and everyone said she looked like Annette Funicello from the Mickey Mouse Club. And everyone in Botany wondered what she was doing with me.

One day I told Pam I was going to run away and not come back until my mother returned. She wanted to run away too so I sold my drum kit and we hit the road. Didn't work. After we ran out of money, she had to call her parents. Her dad came and got us. My poor dad didn't even know I was gone. As soon as we got back, Pam's dad barred me from ever seeing her again.

With no girl, no job, and no drums, I soon started work in another factory, and another, and another. I don't know how many jobs I had that first year but when I did my tax return, they wouldn't all fit on the form. You could start a job in the morning and if you didn't like it leave at little lunch. Walk to another factory and start in the afternoon. I did spend a bit of time at a Chamois factory, but as always, after a while, I moved on.

I tried an Aerosol Factory where I was the only male.mainly because Pam worked there and I could see her so long as her parents didn't find out. By the end of the day I smelt sickly sweet from all the perfumes and stuff. The women used to enjoy telling me rude jokes to watch me blush. I didn't even know ladies knew swears words and talked stuff like that. I didn't last, I just couldn't handle the smart remarks at Bill's Milk Bar when my mates caught a whiff of me.

5

1957   BEXLEY

One day my father announced the house in Hale Street was sold. We were
to leave for Bexley. I was horrified, Bexley was miles away. Though in truth it
wasn't far. I think the move may have been in progress before the split.
Something to do with my ever worsening asthma.

After a while I started an apprenticeship with Enoch Taylor Shoes at their
big factory a couple of streets from Hale Street. I could have walked there in
a few minutes had we still lived in Botany. From Bexley it took three buses,
including of all things, a trolley bus.

Later that year I bought my first motorbike. It was just an old Triumph
Thunderbird, but I thought it was neat. I reckoned from then on, I'd be riding
to work in style. No more buses for Geoffrey Grocott. Things didn't quite
work out that way as half the time I couldn't even start it. I hadn't a clue
mechanically and didn't keep an eye on the oil levels, amongst other things.
One day the motor seized. Back to the buses for a spell.

Working in Botany meant I could sneak out with Pam, sometimes. We had
to be careful as I was still very much on the outer with her parents. At least
my Dad was proud of me. 'Australian made shoes and boots are the best,' he
said. 'Learn the shoe trade and you'll have a job for life.'

Eventually I got the Triumph back complete with a reconditioned engine.
The mechanic showed me how to check the oil and other stuff. I had a lot to

learn.

At lunch time the young workers at T Shoes walked to the nearby Botany shops. No more for me, I had wheels. One rainy day, I was as usual, having great trouble starting my motorbike. My workmates always took great delight in this. 'Want us to bring your lunch back?' they would call out. 'Put a penny in it.' and so on. Finally, and long after they had disappeared around the corner the Triumph roared into life. I took off after them. I didn't know then about motorbikes and wet roads. I was about to learn the hard way.

I flew up the street determined to be the first to the shops. They were nearly to the pub on the corner of Botany Road when I caught up with them. Turned out I had left my run a little late. When I jumped on the back brake, down I went. As I slid across Botany Road on my backside I was thinking, 'Thank god for little gaps in the traffic.'

The Triumph was first to reach the other side of Botany Road first with me close behind. I got to my feet and shook myself to a round of applause from my fellow workmates. The first of many motorcycle mishaps to come.

Things at Bexley weren't going to plan either. Suddenly Dad moved out and Mum moved in. When you're a kid a lot of adult stuff goes over your head. I guess there must have been some contact between my parents, though I never saw or heard it. Or maybe I just didn't want to know. I was back to living with Mum and this time I didn't know where my father was.

Later some people came to stay with us. Their name was Matheson, a country railway couple who had been transferred to Sydney. They had kids with them, and a great uncle who was different. I couldn't figure this Uncle out at all. He acted like a little kid, but he was old. He smelt funny too. Somehow, they all fitted into the Bexley house, and because the great uncle was home all day my red kelpie had a new best friend. I wasn't happy about that either.

I don't know what my mother's relationship with this Mr. Matheson was, though I do remember he was a particularly good looking man. I think they were just work mates and Mum was doing him a favor. At any rate, Mrs. Matheson and Mum got on well.

Somehow my father got wind they were staying with us and one day he stormed into the house demanding answers. Mum was at work. I had never seen my father angry before. I guess he'd just had enough. For all that the Mathesons stayed a while longer.

Uncle, red kelpie and me, watched T.V. on Saturday afternoons. Our favorite was the World Championship Wrestling. We sure loved that show.

One day, while we were watching an old movie, the penny dropped. Our uncle was just like Uncle Dick in David Copperfield. Every bit as sweet and gentle as the one in the novel. At first I resented the Mathesons and their strange relative, adolescent boys are not known for compassion. But little by little I grew to like them, especially my Uncle Dick. I would watch him sometimes as he played with the younger children. He was most comfortable in their world. I never did find out how Uncle Dick came to be living with the Mathesons. Perhaps he was Mrs. Matheson's older brother. I never thought to ask. No matter, they always treated him with the utmost respect.

Eventually the Mathesons found a place to live and moved on. I never saw them again. But for a long time, I missed my Uncle Dick, especially on Saturday arvo when the wrestling was on.

Then my sister and her new husband came to live with us and the man across the road brought home a brand new Holden car. Two toned blue with white wall tyres. He told me he had been on the waiting list a long time. I promised myself I too would have a new car one day. It would be a long time in coming. In the meantime, I had lasted at three months at T. Shoes. A new record.

I continued my travelling to work by bus or bike, depending on the mood of the Triumph. Pam was back in and out of the too hard basket. Then one day out of the blue, Mum announced the Bexley house was sold and we were moving to Mascot. Right next to Botany. Oh, happy days.

6

1958   MASCOT

Our Mascot house was a 100-year-old timber cottage full of character and charm. The original well was still in the middle of the back yard. The cottage was wonderful and creaky. We loved it from day one.

I was back where I belonged. The only thing missing was a motorbike that would start in the morning and for that I needed to earn more money. I applied for a job at the Platypus Leather Tannery in Tenterden Road Botany. When I asked the foreman about my wage he quietly replied, 'Son, we only employ men. Do a man's work, get a man's pay.'

As I badly needed a new motorbike, I did the work. It was hard wet and dirty, but at the end of each week I got a man sized pay packet. That made it all worthwhile.

If I had thought I was woofy at the Aerosol factory, by the end of the day in the tannery I was even woofy-er. If there's such a word. Fortunately, there were plenty of hot showers in the tannery. Most of the men, including me, used them before leaving at the end of the day. Just as well, or the birth rate at Botany would have plummeted. Still, no matter how hard I scrubbed, I always retained the smell of a tannery worker. Even a fast ride home on my motorbike couldn't erase it.

Strange how small the world can be at times. As I walked from the Platypus Tannery that summer day in 1958, I passed a small house three doors down. The house was home to a family of immigrants from Croatia. The Sizgorics. We had never met, but in another time and another place, we would come to know each other, very well.

I was employed to replace Jim who worked the fleshing machine, or as one of the local doctors called it, "The Widow Maker." It wasn't all that bad, though really a job for young men, and Jim was no longer that. Working class people then had a stubborn pride in their work ethic. Botany men were judged by their ability to endure hard toil. When one gossiped about a fellow worker they would often ask, 'And how does he work?' and so on. One day I overheard someone enquiring about me. The answer came, 'Oh he works alright. But he mucks around a lot.'

My day at Platypus usually began with the unloading of a truckload of untreated animal skins direct from the abattoir. Truck drivers then didn't worry much about covering their loads. Locals didn't complain, all part and parcel of living in Botany. Often the flesh left on the hides was full of maggots and it wasn't unusual to find a few strays on your clothing when you were having lunch. On my first day Jim advised me to not worry about the little blokes saying, 'They don't eat much.'

The hides went into a large chemical bath the size of a backyard pool. Next morning I'd haul them out minus hair. I wore a heavy rubber apron and gumboots, but that was about it as far as safety gear went. We were Botany boys; Botany boys were supposed to be tough.

Come Mondays, my first task was to fish out any critters that had fallen in the chemical bath over the weekend. Mostly they were large rats. Very dead, very bloated, and very hairless. That task complete, I'd load my wheelbarrow with hides and start up the fleshing machine. With its large rollers it looked somewhat like a huge version of an old washing machine wringer, excepting the rollers had blades. Noise from motors and pulleys made ordinary speech impossible and shouting was the order of the day.

At lunch the men played Euchre. I listened and learned. A few of them had served in the Second World War, though rarely spoke of it. I gathered there was still some bad blood between them and the shirkers who had used the tannery for an excuse to stay behind. When you work with older men their wisdom and experience change you. I was at last beginning to grow up.

After a while I was invited to join the lunch time card game. My partner was Jim. I had made it.

While my new job was going well, things with the best sort in Botany were sort of up and down. We did see each other, but always on the quiet, and always well away from her dad.

One night the best sort asked me to take her to a waterfront hotel at nearby Sans Souci. A band was playing she liked. Though we were under aged we managed to sneak in and found good seats near the stage.

The band was great. The best sort was having the time of her life. After all the drama of the last year or so, it was great to see her enjoying herself. She sure loved that band.

Later a waiter handed my girl a small piece of paper.

'What was that?' I asked the best sort in Botany.

'Oh, just something I dropped,' she said smiling as she popped it in her purse.

Everything was well on the way home. She'd had a good night. I loved to see her happy.

I didn't hear from her for a few days but that wasn't unusual, especially if her dad was in one of his hate Geoffrey moods. Perhaps she'd been grounded for coming home late after our night out. Or worse still, her father had discovered she'd committed the ultimate sin by going out with me.

The next weekend I wandered in to our local fish and chipper. There to my surprise was the best sort in Botany. With a smile I walked over but to my horror she looked right through me. I didn't know what I had done wrong and as she sure wasn't about to tell me, I high tailed it out of there.

A week later, I heard the best sort in Botany was going out with some singer in a band. Yes, that band.

Single again I worked every bit of overtime on offer and before long I had the deposit for an almost new Triumph Tiger 110. I figured it would be a fair

14

replacement for my ex-girl, and a whole lot less trouble.

There was one other problem. The tattoo of a heart on my forearm with "Pam" smack right in the middle. Oh well I thought, one day I might meet another Pam. I never did.

A little later, I heard on the grapevine the thing with the best sort and the older man, a.k.a. the singer, hadn't gone all that well. At times, I would see Pam around Botany. She looked good but I kept my distance. I no longer had the need for a girlfriend, I was in love with my Tiger 110.

Jim lived just around the corner from me, often I would give him a lift to work. I liked Jim; he was different to the other tannery workers. I could feel he was educated and at times wondered why he worked at Platypus. I was sure he had done better things. But Jim was tight lipped about his past, and it remained a mystery to me.

Later I found out Jim's doctor had informed his wife if he didn't slow up, would be curtains. Soon after Mrs. Jim had a secret meeting with the foreman. A short time later Jim was told his talents were needed elsewhere in the tannery.

Sometimes Jim came over to watch me work his "Widow Maker". He seemed to approve.

We must have made a strange sight on our way to work. Jim, the well-dressed older man with me, casual, and often shoeless. Few wore helmets then and I certainly didn't. I was far too clever for that sensible sort of stuff.

Later when I got a motorbike and sidecar, Jim was happier and even learned to lean out a little on the left handers.

I was content. A well-paid job, nice motorbike, this was as good as it got for Botany Boys like me. I had no further ambitions. As far as I was concerned, Botany was the centre of the world.

That year I made a new friend. Jeff Chen, a local kid who also rode a Triumph Tiger 110. That was how we got around to talking in the first place. We spent most weekends cruising around on our bikes. Jeff was a trainee accountant, or something like that. He worked in the city and at times I would see him on his way to the office. Jeff looked smart in his suit and tie. Bit different to my work attire.

Jeff went to the Showground Speedway most Saturday nights but for some reason I never joined him. Perhaps I still hadn't recovered from my night there with the Warren family.

Jeff's parents were well to do Chinese. They lived in a lovely home on upmarket Tunstall Avenue, Kensington overlooking the Australian Golf Course. Prosperous and hardworking, the Chen family didn't appreciate their only son riding a motorbike. Nor did they care for the friend who smelt a little like one of those awful tanneries you passed on the way to the airport. Not that they ever got close enough to get a good whiff. I never so much as made it past the front gate. I cannot remember one time they even acknowledged my existence. To them I was invisible, or they wished I was and for the first time, I realised I was from the wrong side of the tracks. Still, if you rode a motorbike in the late fifties, you grew accustomed to being on the outer. Every time you ventured on the streets you were pulled over and harassed by some traffic policeman. Didn't matter if every second car had a drunk behind the wheel. As they often did. We motorcycle hoodlums were to be dealt with.

After a movie called the Wild One, starring Marlon Brando, was released, one of Sydney's high-ranking police officers decided that sort of behavior would not be tolerated. Apparently, someone forgot to inform him it was only make believe. From then on, the humble motorcycle and their riders were enemy number one. Though in truth, we were only number two. The real public enemy number one reserved for homosexuals.

In 1957, our beloved Police Commissioner announced, 'Homosexuals were the greatest menace facing Australians.' Under his watch convictions had increased by an outstanding sixty six percent. Thanks to him we could sleep safe in our beds. Oh, except for the Brando copycats. A further blitz was ordered, we were to be hounded from the streets. Heaven help should you be gay and ride a motorcycle. Perhaps he was right. I distinctly remember Jeff Chen consuming two chocolate malts in one night. Totally out of control.

By then Jeff was my best friend. Perhaps because he was a little wild like me, and had a keen sense of humour. We made a good pair.

One day, and on a whim, Jeff and I decided to visit my brother Jimmy in faraway outback Moree. The P.M.G. department transferred him there not long after he started his apprenticeship. That was how they did things then.

We decided to travel on one bike, with one change of clothes. Jeff reckoned Moree couldn't be all that far. We were soon to soon find out, it was indeed far.

16

We reached Gunnedah late the first afternoon. Had a bite to eat, then headed out of town to find a camp spot. The nights were warm in the early summer. We were keen to sleep under the stars.

We rode until it was almost dusk. As night fell, hundreds of kangaroos appeared from nowhere. After a few near misses we settled for a good spot under a huge gum tree to make camp. Jeff was having the time of his life.

'We'll be in Moree tomorrow,' he proudly announced before adding, 'Too easy.' Just one of his regular sayings.

The next day we made Narrabri by mid-morning. Everything was going swimmingly.

As we rode into town I noticed some puddles on the side of the road and thought to myself, 'Glad the rains stopped.'

We took our time, had some food and wandered the main street. It was only about sixty miles to Moree. We didn't feel the need to hurry. We'd be there for lunch. Jeff was right, it was all too easy.

A few miles out of town the road changed to dirt. I had the handlebars and Jeff yelled in my ear, 'Don't worry, this won't last long.' We were city kids, we didn't know anything about riding on dirt.

After a while the dirt began to change colour. From a sort of brown to black. At first, we thought we were back on the bitumen. Then down we went.

After sliding a heck of a long way, we came to a halt smack in the middle of a large puddle. I looked back for Jeff, we'd parted company as soon as we hit the deck. He was alright, just laughing his head off as usual. I tried to pick up the Triumph, but as soon as it was upright I went over again, 'What is this black stuff?'

Jeff thought it all very amusing. 'Ah, too funny, too funny,' he yelled. Another of his many sayings.

We cleaned the mud off the bike, and us, then resumed our journey. This time with Jeff on the bars. He reckoned because he watched the Speedway every Saturday night, he knew how to handle dirt.

A few hundred yards later we went down again. At this stage, Jeff was still laughing. 'I think I've got the hang of it now,' he assured me.

We did last a little longer the next time, and the next. Then I tried the handlebars. Same result.

'Maybe we should go back to Narrabri,' I said, but Jeff only laughed. He

17

was sure the bitumen was just over the next rise. Was he right? I didn't know. Anyway, I sure didn't feel like riding back looking the way we did. They would probably lock us up.

Turned out we'd gone the wrong way. A wet black soil road was no place for a motorbike with two dumb city kids.

We didn't even make the outskirts of Moree that night. Exhausted, dirty and hungry, we slept by the side of the road. When the sun rose, we found a creek and washed some of the black mud from the bike, and us. Overnight the road had dried a little so we managed to ride the last few miles without incident. At long last we limped into Moree.

Safe in Jimmy's flat, Jeff and I tossed for the first shower. After we had cleaned up the hunger pains set in. We headed for town, minus the Tiger 110.

After a great meal in a Greek café, we stopped to sit awhile on the town hall steps. The warmth of the sun, and the events of the last two days soon had us drowsy. Before long we were both fast asleep. I'm not sure how long we slept but I awoke to find two big policemen shaking us. We were still half asleep as they dragged us to our feet and marched us to a waiting Paddy Wagon. We protested our innocence to whatever it was they thought we had done but all to no avail. In we went and the door slammed hard behind us. Inside was standing room only, most of the other occupants seemed to be local aborigines.

Suddenly the van lurched going around a corner. Jeff lost his footing and for a moment I thought we were in trouble. Turned out Jeff couldn't fall far, wasn't enough room. Anyway, there was no need to worry as the lads were in a happy mood. They helped Jeff to his feet and asked our names, and where we'd come from. We filled them in on our trip. The slippery black soil and the other stuff. Wasn't strange to them that a chocolate malt and a hamburger had landed us in the slammer. Seemed every afternoon a Paddy Wagon cruised the Moree streets. Anyone who looked out of place or under the weather was picked up for a sleep and a sober up if necessary. The next morning most were released until the next time. There didn't appear to be any hard feelings on either side.

We arrived at the police station. Jeff and I stumbled out onto the footpath with our new friends. This time we didn't bother protesting our innocence thinking surely by now they would have realised their mistake. They had not, so we quietly followed our new friends into the waiting cell. All the while I was thinking, 'If Jeff's parents ever hear about this, I won't even make it into Tunstall Avenue when we get back.' That's if we ever got back. Moree was beginning to feel a long way from home.

Eventually, and after much pleading, a constable rang Jimmy. We left town early the next morning.

Jimmy showed us another road. 'Sealed all the way,' he said. And that was true, except for the one small stretch they were working on. Someone had forgot to put out a warning sign. When we picked up the bike, the only damage was to our clean clothes. 'Ah, too funny, too funny,' laughed Jeff and I had to agree.

We took a detour to have a look at my Mum's hometown, then rode onto Bathurst for a lap around Mt. Panorama. All the while imagining ourselves boy racers. We made a promise to return next Easter to watch the annual bike races but that was never to happen. A few weeks later Jeff met a girl. I didn't see him much after that. I guess that made his parents happy. I went back to riding alone.

7

1959 BONDI BEACH

One Sunday I took a ride to Bondi Beach. As I cruised down Hall Street, I passed a milk bar that seemed to have half of Sydney's motorbikes out front. It was a warm day; I could smell the sea. Motorbikes or surf? I did a U-turn.

That simple turn would change my life forever. And the lives of Johnny Dunne and Teddy Preston. Rosemary Lee's life too was changed that day. I often wonder how my life, and theirs, would have turned out had I just ridden on.

I parked the Triumph and walked inside to a scene from Happy Days. Girls dancing, jukebox blaring, lots of teenagers having a good time. I ordered a double chocolate malt and checked the dance floor. There was this skinny girl with a big smile that caught my eye, and boy could she dance. I heard someone say her name was Rosemary. She didn't have eyes for me though, and it was Renee who walked over and introduced herself.

By the end of that day I had a whole new bunch of friends. They were all going for a ride to the Royal National Park the next Sunday and I was invited. Renee liked the look of my Tiger 110, and that was fine by me because I sure

20

liked the look of her. Renee lived at Maroubra where her family had a food business, but I was to pick her up around the corner as her dad didn't like motorbikes, or their Aussie riders. A nice Greek boy was what he had in mind. I didn't care, I was used to being on the outer.

It sure felt good cruising around Sydney with my new friends. There were about ten of us, most with their girlfriends riding pillion. Some of the blokes lived around the inner Sydney suburb of Newtown, not far from my home at Mascot. During the week, they hung out at the "High Society" hamburger joint in Newtown's main street. It became my regular haunt.

Johnny Dunne, the sort of "Leader of the pack" was going out Carol, a girl I knew from Mascot. She lived with her mum in an old house where the long term airport car park now stands. Johnnie's best mate was Teddy Preston from nearby Waterloo. The three of us hit it off.

Johnny lived in Alice Street Newtown and worked at the nearby Coca Cola plant. Teddy drove a forklift for the British Motor Corporation in Zetland. He would never leave he once told me.

Johnny along with his brother and sister lived on the second floor of a rundown old Newtown mansion while Ted lived in a housing commission terrace. Sadly, Ted and his family were about to be moved to a new public housing estate at far away Villawood. All part and parcel of the State Government's grand plan to relocate inner city housing commission tenants out west. Along with his mother and an older brother, they were moved in the middle of a hot Sydney summer to a sort of a newly built semi-detached house in the then treeless far western Sydney suburb of Villawood. In the early sixties, the area had little in the way of facilities, but as with everything, Ted took it all in his stride. His only concern was for his mum. I felt sorry for Teddy having to move so far out, little did I know in a couple of years I too would follow. Ted's father Joe, a World War Two veteran, stayed behind at Waterloo. In the Perry Keyes song, "The day John Sattler broke his jaw", he laments how they cleared the inner city dwellers from their terrace houses with the line, "They sent you out to Campbelltown, Mount Druitt and St. Marys." John Sattler was a legendary South Sydney rugby league player who bravely played on in a Rugby League grand final with a broken jaw. Today most of the terraces are home to the well off, and much of that early culture, good or bad lost forever.

We certainly weren't three peas in pod. John was tall, good looking, and moody, while the ever-smiling Teddy resembled a big cuddly bear. Then there was me, the kid with the crew cut and crooked teeth who always mucked around.

John seemed to have a chip on his shoulder, perhaps over his parents, though he never explained. And while John remained tight lipped, his eyes at times showed the pain. John could be unpredictable but if he decided you were his friend; he would move mountains for you. Heaven help if you were the enemy.

Ted was different. No chip on his big shoulders. Nor grudges. I cannot remember even one time he spoke ill of anyone. Ted's job on the forklift at British Motor Corporation was one of the most important things in his life. Growing up in poverty stricken Waterloo, he had watched the drunks and no hopers blow their money in pubs and S.P. betting shops. Early on, Teddy promised himself he would never be one of those. The only time I can recall seeing Teddy angry was when somebody made a smart remark about his mother's new partner. He soon calmed down.

By then I had gotten over my parent's break up. Though I still didn't understand what drove my mother to leave, I tried to put it out of my mind. I would have dearly loved to have my father back home, but that's how it was. I still lived in my own little dream world and still hadn't got over the day my sister and I discovered Christmas presents hidden in a cupboard. I was confused until she slowly said, 'Geoff, there is no Santa Claus.'

Only Mum and I lived in the old house at Mascot. Dad was in a boarding house near the city. We met up one night for a meal in a café just around the corner from my old school in Cleveland Street, Surry Hills. The area then wasn't the trendy suburb of to-day, more the gritty home of Ruth Park novels.

The café was a simple affair that catered for the many lonely singles from the area's cheap boarding houses. Better to meet there and save us the embarrassment of seeing where he was forced to live. *The food wasn't too bad and I still remember the sign on a wall that went something like, "I used to complain about no shoes. Then I saw a man with no feet."*

We made uncomfortable small talk. Dad asked how things were in the Tannery. Did I know he was retiring soon, and so on?

I told him about my trip to Moree to see Jimmy, but didn't mention the slammer and falling off stuff.

22

When we parted, there was a sadness in his eyes that ripped right through me. If only I could have taken him back to the bush. I held my tears until I rode away on the Tiger 110. No need for the damaged war hero to see his youngest son cry.

8

1960   SPEEDWAY and COCA COLA

One night over a chocolate malt at Bondi Beach, the skinny girl with the smile walked over and chatted. After a while I asked if she wanted to go to the pictures at Botany. She had never heard of Botany so I offered to show her a little more of the world. Anyway, Renee was about to flick me, something to do with the way I smelt. At that stage the skinny girl thought the leathery aroma was from my new leather jacket. Her name was Rosemary, and of course her family didn't like motorcycle riders, particularly those who hung around milk bars drinking chocolate malted milkshakes. As usual I didn't make it past the front gate. Different story at my place, Mum welcomed the skinny girl with open arms. She reckoned Rosemary had cow's eyes and coming from Mum that was quite a compliment. Perhaps the skinny girl reminded Mum of her long lost milking cow. At any rate, they hit it off from day one.

One Saturday night Rosemary and I were at a loose end. Everyone else was off doing something or other. We were riding back from Bondi when I saw the bright lights of the Sydney Showgrounds. I was

'Want to go to the speedway?' I yelled over my shoulder.

'What's that?'

'Motorbike racing. Cars too.'

'Yuk.'

'Good food.'

'Oh, alright.'

As we rode in, crowds of people were making their way to the spectator areas. It was too late to get a seat in the stands so we settled for one of the grassed areas. Things hadn't changed much since my last visit as a ten year old, except maybe I had grown up a little. When the pit gates opened for the first race, I watched fascinated as the riders started their machines and moved to the start line. Under the bright track lights they reminded me of the Gladiators from ancient Rome. As the starting tapes flew high the ground lights went out leaving only the riders and the track illuminated. They still tore round at breakneck speed, but this time I couldn't take my eyes off them. By the end of the meeting I had decided to become a speedway rider. I had no idea how one went about becoming a speedway rider, but I wasn't going to let a little thing like that stop me. It was the sidecar racers that caught my eye. I watched in awe as they wrestled their big Vincent powered machines around the track. I sure wanted to be one of them.

The next day I thought it might be a good idea to actually learn how ride a motorcycle and sidecar before I attempted to become a Speedway Sidecar star. Rosemary and I had just bought a new Triumph Bonneville, I had to convince her that we needed to attach a sidecar to her pride and joy. Reluctantly she gave her permission and a few weeks later I proudly pushed our Bonneville with its newly fitted Aussie made Tilbrook sidecar into our street. I did try to ride it back from the local workshop but I kept running off the road. After a while I gave up and pushed it the rest of the way home. It wasn't far, only about a mile.

Johnny and Teddy were waiting patiently to see me make my entrance. They cracked up when I came into view sheepishly pushing the motorcycle and sidecar. By then I had talked them into coming to the speedway, and like me they were excited by the exciting new world. Ted jumped in the sidecar saying all it needed was a passenger and we'd be right. Again, I tried to make the Bonny go in a straight line, and again it would not. Then Johnny tried. Then Teddy again. Still the bloody thing wouldn't go where it was supposed. What chance would we have to be sidecar stars if we couldn't even ride down our street?

Mum had been watching our antics and joined in. 'I used to have a boyfriend with a motorcycle and sidecar,' she offered. 'I rode it once. I remember him saying you had to steer it like a car.'

Mum jumped on the Bonneville and rode slowly up the street, did a U-turn and rode back. We clapped and cheered, and we laughed and we laughed. Mum had saved the day, and at that moment I knew, despite all that had happened, I still loved my mum dearly.

I often think of those long ago summer days. Of Johnny and Teddy, laughing, mucking around with motorbikes. Best friends forever!

Jim got quite a shock on Monday morning when I pulled in front of his house on the Bonneville and sidecar. He didn't hesitate, just smiled and jumped in. This was so much better than riding pillion, there was even a small windscreen to keep the dust off.

By then I knew my time at the Platypus Tannery was coming to an end as Rosemary had long since realised my woofyness wasn't due to a new leather jacket. She wanted her future husband to meet her family, and no amount of deodorant would ever hide my occupation. But I was reluctant to take another job, or work away from Botany. I felt secure at Platypus. I liked my job. I liked my workmates. It had taken a long time to earn their respect, I didn't want them to think I thought myself too good for the tannery. For a long time Johnny had pestered me to join him working nights at the Coca Cola plant. I reluctantly made the move.

On my last day, Jim shook my hand saying, 'If I could work the fleshing machine, I could ride one of them speedway bikes.' He expected to see my name in the paper one day.

I played my last card game and walked away. There was no send off, Botany boys didn't have time for that stuff. I hung up my apron, handed back the gumboots, and that was that.

••••

As far as I was concerned, the Coca Cola plant in Rickety Road at Mascot, only had one thing going for it. It was close to home. My shift started at 11pm and finished next morning at 7. Boring monotonous factory work, night after night. No working-class culture, no mucking around, just men going through the motions while dreaming of being somewhere else. Most were recent immigrants trying to get ahead in their new country. They worked day jobs as well, leaving them little time or energy to play my games. To them I was just another crazy lazy Australian. So boring all this serious stuff. I missed my friends at Platypus, and most of all I missed their dry Aussie humour.

Eventually Johnny and I did break the ice a little with the new Aussies and in time came to understand them. I'm not sure they ever came to understand me.

Life at the Coca Cola plant went as follows; half an hour sitting in front of a light checking the empty bottles coming from the wash on a conveyor belt. Remove any stuff stuck in them and in another half an hour later change with the bloke on other side. There I would place the now filled bottles, four at a time, into wooden crates. The only Coca Cola product then was the small glass bottles of black coke, Fanta would come next. Another half an hour and it was back to the light, and on and on it went.

After a while I became the dinner boy and that gave me a chance to get away every night. If only for a short while. The closest food place was the "High Society" in King Street Newtown. Maybe it wasn't closest, but it was for me. Jack the owner appreciated the business and sometimes Teddy and a few of our friends would be there.

I don't remember how long I lasted at Coca Cola. A few months maybe, all the while trying to work up the courage to tell Johnny I just didn't feel about the place as he did. I longed to be back at the tannery with the Botany blokes, smell or no smell. But I knew John would be hurt if I went elsewhere, loyalty was everything to him. He thought he had done me a good turn; my leaving would be a personal insult. Fortunately, John got a promotion to drive forklifts on the day shift and that let me off the hook. Still, he wasn't happy with my going, but I made the excuse of it being no fun if I had to do nights on my own.

'Look at me,' Johnny proudly said. 'See what can happen if you stay at Coca Cola.'

Johnny was so pleased with his promotion. He was going places like Teddy, while all I could think of was the Platypus Leather Tannery and downtown Botany.

In the end I left Coca Cola and John was pretty cool with me for a while. I heard they were having trouble getting someone to last on the fleshing machine and figured I could walk straight back in. But Rosemary put her foot down. There'd be no more tanneries, no more Botany, she had seen a notice for a storeman at nearby Leyland Motors and insisted I apply. Yuk. What does a storeman do I wondered? To keep her happy I called in. Bugger, I started the next day.

That summer I spent every Saturday night at the Showground studying the sidecar racers. My favourite was Doug Robson, he seemed somehow different to the others, and boy could he ride.

One night as I hung around the pit gates, I saw Doug Robson without his helmet. He wasn't much older than me, but he sure was handsome. Doug Robson really did look like a gladiator.

Each week after the bike races finished, I'd walk to the pit gate to watch as the riders loaded their bikes and gear. I was far too shy to ask any questions, anyway they were usually too busy signing autographs to notice me. Nearby was a stall where you could buy pictures of the stars. I bought a few of Doug Robson. When I showed them to my niece Karen she said, 'Uncle Geoff, that man looks like Elvis Presley.' And so he did.

I noticed Doug Robson rarely socialized with other riders. At the end of the bike races his pit crew loaded the magnificent Vincent HRD and off he drove. On the front of his bike was a small plate with the initials AGR. That didn't make sense to me, I wondered what it meant.

Reluctantly Rosemary and I sold our Triumph Bonneville as we needed a utility to cart our speedway bike to meetings. Not that we had a speedway bike. All we had was one well used 650cc Triumph engine, a copy of Phil Irving's book "Tuning for Speed", and great expectations.

A good friend, Harry Ross, volunteered to be my passenger after we met at the High Society milk bar and clicked. Harry was a good bloke, who like me lived alone with his mum. I spent a lot of time at their inner city Marrickville home. Though we didn't have a race bike, that minor detail hadn't stopped us buying leathers, boots, and such.

One day we dressed in our racing gear to parade for Harry's mum. She thought we looked good, as did my mum the next day. All that was missing was a speedway bike. But where to find one?

I placed an ad in a motorcycle magazine, "Wanted. One Speedway outfit, with or without motor." There was no response and I was left wondering what to do next.

In the meantime, my job at Leyland Motors was going well and I had to admit it was nice arriving home without a tannery aroma. George, the head store man took me under his wing and I learned lots about the motor trade, and life. It was good to have an older man mentoring me, though even George couldn't convince me to give away my dream of one day becoming a speedway rider.

British Leyland was a truck and bus manufacturer, we dispatched replacement parts all over the state. I discovered I was a quick learner with a good memory for numbers and despite my initial doubts I was beginning to enjoy this new life.

Early one Friday night I answered a knock at our front door. Standing before me was my idol Doug Robson. I was gob smacked. He said he had come about my advertisement but it had to be a dream. Doug Robson would never come to my place. Indeed, the great man was standing right in front of me, and I knew whatever he had for sale I would buy, and at any price. Doug Robson would never cheat.

Turned out Doug was a straight shooter, and had just what we needed. Best of all he seemed to like me, I was invited to his home the next afternoon to watch his team prepare for the night's meeting. I asked Doug would it be alright if I brought my girl along. That was okay too. Later I thought maybe it wasn't such a good idea, especially after Pam and the singer stuff. Doug Robson was much better looking than the singer. Turned out I didn't have to worry as he already had a girl. Her name was Glenda, she and Rosemary hit it off as well.

It was the first of many days I would
spend with my idol Doug Robson. But as
with many long and close friendships,
along the way would come some rain.

I had finally made it into the Showground pits, all thanks to my new best friend, sidecar star Douglas Robson. I was on my way.

And things were happening at Leland Motors. I was offered a promotion to the Parts Sales Department. A collar and tie job. It seemed only weeks before I was at the Platypus Tannery flicking maggots off my sandwiches. Of course Rosemary was pleased, at last she could take me home to meet her mother.

9

1961

As the summer of 61 came to an end, the Showground Speedway, as always, made way for the annual Royal Easter Show. With our Triumph Speedway Sidecar at last ready, we nominated to ride at the Westmead Showground for the winter months. Luckily, they were a little short of riders, meaning we didn't have to wait for a place on the program.

I had been studying the sidecar riders for so long, it seemed somehow normal to be out there amongst them. After a couple of practice laps, we nervously lined up for the first heat of the sidecar handicap, starting from scratch. We actually led for a lap, then the back markers began to overtake us. I wasn't prepared for the dirt spraying from their back wheels. One minute all was clear. next everything turned to black. Then suddenly it was daylight again, Harry had changed my gas goggles.

Going into the last lap we were still third until a flying Doug Robson came past, sideways. The dirt from the other riders was minor to what Doug's big Vincent hit us. Again, Harry came to the rescue and quickly changed my goggles and I watched in awe as Doug forced his way past the two leaders to go on and win. We came in fourth. I had a lot to learn.

Later we rode in the consolation race and hung on for a third while Doug had his usual big day winning the star's scratch race and handicap final. He walked over at the end of the meet and said quietly, 'Better bring your bike around next Saturday, needs some setting up.' And with that he was off, just another race day for Doug Robson.

By then Teddy's outfit was almost ready and John was about to buy a solo. I was the first of us to race on a speedway track, beating them by a few months.

A couple of weeks later I had my first crash when another rider spun in front of us. We hit their sidecar and sailed high in the air. Harry and I were uninjured, not so our bike. But we were back the next week. That accident was our first test as lots of budding speedway riders last only till their first accident and are never seen again.

After a few more meetings, I thought I'd try to gain a little extra speed for the big Westmead track. The Triumph's cylinders were bored to the maximum and a set of super high compression pistons thrown in. Everything was good for a couple of meetings until the cylinders let go with a mighty bang. Back to the drawing board. I knew we needed a Vincent H.R.D. and there was only one thing stopping us. Money, or lack thereof, I started saving.

One Sunday afternoon, my father came to the Westmead Showgrounds wandering into the pits just before the start. Dad looked out of place in his hat, coat and tie. A man from another time. The track was particularly rough that day. All Dad could find to say was, 'Geoff. Surely you're not going to ride on that track?' But of course I did, and as far as I know it was the only time my father ever came to a speedway meeting. A few months earlier he was shocked when I asked him to sign my application for a speedway licence. The look on my father's face had said it all. He shook his head and frowned, then said, 'You're not going to ride Speedway?' I guess after all Dad had experienced, he wondered why I would risk life and limb for what to him was just a motorcycle race. But they were easy times. The "Happy Days", when kids like me thought they could do anything and nothing would ever change. My father's life had been the opposite, leaving him quiet and cautious. I sometimes wonder what my father really thought of his youngest son that winter Sunday at the Westmead Speedway. I'm sure he would have rather I played cricket, his favourite sport. And while cricket would have been a lot simpler, after I copped a bouncer at Banksmeadow Public I lost all interest in the game.

The young Fred Grocott had risked all in
WW1. Not for sport, for duty. His

grandparents were British, the home country was in peril. Three young Grocott brothers joined the A.I.F and set off for the other side of the world.

Because of a house fire I have few photos of my father. One has him in a group of young soldiers taken just before embarking. Best mate Jimmy Field by his side. Country kids off to do their part. Reality, country kids off to be cannon fodder in a faraway obscene war between cousins.

....

Harry and I had mixed success in our first season. Lots of bike trouble, peppered with a few encouraging wins. We did gain a few yards in handicap rating, though not enough to earn a start at the Showground for the coming summer season. With the imminent closure of the Westmead circuit due to its being the site for a new children's hospital, our speedway future looked bleak. There were rumours of an all-new speedway track being constructed near the Kembla Grange horse racing course on the NSW South Coast. We waited. By then Rosemary and I were engaged with our marriage planned for the following March. Rosemary worked in the office of the Australian Railways Union. Being a railway woman, my mum liked that. She was proud of her future daughter-in-law. And, Rosemary's parents had finally accepted the inevitable. At long last I was invited into their Bondi Beach home.

Rosemary's twin, Robin, ventured out to Westmead one day to see me in action. I had a lousy meeting and we wasn't impressed, later suggesting to his sister, 'I don't think Geoff has much of a future as a speedway rider.'

The Railways Union was just down the road from my old school in Cleveland Street. The open air ice skating rink in Prince Alfred Park was close. Two things Rosemary loved were skating and dancing. Often, we'd go to the rink at night. She was graceful, I was hopeless, we skated at opposite ends. Mostly I just hung to the fence watching her glide past.

While my new life at Leyland Motors was going well, I began to dream how good it would be to have a similar job in the motorcycle business. There was no great future in motorcycles at that time as only a handful of motorcycle businesses remained in the city and suburbs. The cheap and reliable lightweight bikes from Japan were still few, and not that impressive. The anti-motorcycle campaign had taken its toll. Anyone who rode a motorcycle was often regarded with suspicion. Still, the idea of working in a motorcycle shop remained my ultimate dream.

As I had no hope of making the Sydney Showground that summer, I thought if the opportunity arose, I would try my hand as passenger. It turned out I didn't have long to wait long when Wally Smith, a showground rider, asked me to do a few meetings with him at the Windsor track on the outskirts of Sydney. If I did well, I could ride with him at the Sydney Showground.

Wally was a big bloke who had been around sidecars for some time, and was affectionately known in speedway as the Big Bopper. The real Big Bopper, an American D.J. turned singer songwriter, had a one hit wonder named Chantilly Lace. In a way, Wally resembled him, hence the name. Later the original Bopper was killed in the plane crash that also took the lives of Buddy Holly and Ritchie Valens. As things turned out that Sunday afternoon it was fortunate Wally and I didn't join them. It seemed that Wally had a something wrong with one of eyes, though I didn't think it could be much of a problem as he'd been competing for some time.

When I arrived at the track, Wally showed me two pairs of matching silver boots. Very daring for the time. Black was the usual colour for leathers and boots. To wear anything else invited comments on your sexuality. None of this worried the Bopper though. 'Put these on,' he commanded. 'Speedway's showbiz. Ya gotta get noticed.' I thought then maybe Wally really was the reincarnation of the Big Bopper.

I put on the silver boots and they didn't look all that bad. Teddy and Johnny were there, and though they said nothing about the silver boots, every time I looked their way I noticed sly smirks.

The Bopper and I didn't go too good in our first race. The track was wet and slippery, but the Bopper told me not to worry, he would handle it. In the second lap of our second race, the leading outfit suddenly lost it and spun to a halt. The rest of the field somehow managed to avoid the stricken pair. Not the Bopper. He still had the big Vincent on full stick.

Later I saw a picture in a magazine that was taken a moment before contact. There's me with a look of terror, while the Bopper is as cool as Willy the Penguin. Seemed the stalled bike was in his blind spot. We hit hard. The Vincent flew high into the air and eventually returned to earth minus the front forks. I landed some twenty feet further down the track, Bopper came down beside me with a thud. It was quite a day.

When Bopper came back from the hospital, I said I thought I would give the passenger thing a rest for a while. That was okay by him as it was going to be some time before he and the Vincent would again be ready for action.

I handed back the silver boots and went home with Rosemary. She had to drive as I had a few sprains and things. Rosemary remarked she hadn't been all that impressed with my passenger debut.

So, I returned to my spectator role at the Showgrounds dreaming of the night my turn would surely come. I figured once the new track at Kembla Grange opened I would soon gain enough experience to finally make it onto the Golden Bowl.

Then came the Saturday I had a call from Doug Robson. He had just sacked his regular passenger and urgently needed me to ride that night. I didn't ask why. This was my big chance, so what did I care? I was to be at Doug's place that afternoon at one o'clock sharp. I hurried over.

Speedway afternoons at the Robson house always followed a regular routine. First, Doug, his passenger and pit crew shared a late lunch prepared by his mum and fiancé Glenda. Following lunch, the Vincent was fired up for a final check then it was on to the Sydney Showgrounds.

That day I finally worked up the courage to ask Doug why the letters AGR were written on the front of his Vincent. Doug quietly explained they were the initials of his younger brother Alan who had lost his life in a car accident a few years before. Since then, and before every meeting, Doug called into the Rookwood Cemetery to lay flowers on Alan's grave. On leaving he would take two of the flowers and drive quietly on. At the Speedway, and changed into his riding gear, Doug would place a flower in the top of his left boot. His passenger the same. On the way to the start line Doug would reach down to pat his flower, passenger likewise. Doug Robson never varied the ritual. He had never recovered from the loss of his brother and best friend, perhaps it explained why he was a loner.

Alan, a Navy recruit, purchased the Vincent for Doug and him to race together. It was never to be and Doug continued on alone determined to do his best in Alan's memory. For Doug Robson, the championship winning

1000cc Vincent HRD speedway sidecar, would always remain the property of the young sailor, Alan Graham Robson.

I watched on as Doug and his crew went through the usual preparations. Then the big moment as they bump started the sidecar outfit in the driveway. There is nothing quite like the sound and smell of a highly tuned Vincent V twin running on Methanol Fuel and Castrol R oil. A sort of a cross between a Harley Davidson and a machine gun.

We listened as Doug tweaked the throttle. Everything sounded good to my inexperienced ears. But the champ was not happy. He stopped the engine, thought for a while, then unscrewed the spark plugs. After carefully looking at them Doug announced, 'It will have to come out.'

'What will?' we chorused.

'The engine. Something's not right.'

And out it came.

As Doug and his crew frantically dismantled the Vincent engine, I could do nothing but stand and watch. After a while I began to relax. It was after four, no way would we be racing that night. From Doug's home it was at least an hour's drive to the Showgrounds and then we had to make our way through the crowd.

At last the engine was on the workshop bench. When the cylinder heads were removed, he quickly found the problem. One loose valve seat. An hour later the bike was on the trailer. We were on our way.

I thought we would rush as fast as possible to the Showgrounds. But Doug Robson would never race without first visiting Alan.

We drove into the cemetery and Doug stopped to buy flowers. At the gravesite he stood in silence. You could have heard a pin drop.

We did make the Showground before our first race, just. By then my nerves were completely shot as I'd come to realise exactly what I had let myself in for. There would be no practice run. Doug Robson didn't believe in such trivialities. He was a professional, as I was expected to be.

Our first race was a handicap heat. We'd be starting from the back mark of 120 yards behind the front outfit.

On our way to the line Doug patted Alan's flower and motioned me to do the same. That calmed me a little. Anyway, I could hardly jump off in front of twenty thousand people.

As we came to our mark I looked to the stand where I knew Rosemary would be looking on. All I could see was a sea of faces but I nodded anyway. With a firm grip on the side car's hand holds I waited for the inevitable, my heart pumping.

The Vincent's revs slowly increased to a crescendo, then suddenly the green lights went out and Doug dropped the clutch.

It's hard to describe the sensation when a big Vincent Speedway outfit accelerates from the starting line. You need all your strength just to prevent being thrown off.

We roared into the first corner at full speed and somehow I managed to pull myself onto the seat behind Doug. Up ahead I could see five snarling sliding sidecars, their dirt spraying everywhere.

As we raced up the back straight, I noticed Doug was shaking his head. He was filled in dirt and couldn't see properly. I quickly changed his goggles. Everything was a blur. We were passing under bikes and around the outside line inches from the concrete fence. Sideways most of the time. Suddenly it was over. We had finished in second place. The longest 68 seconds of my life.

Back in the pits I expected at least a pat on the back for my first go. But Doug Robson didn't do small talk. 'Too slow with the goggles boy,' was all he had to say. 'I should have won that race.'

I went over to a quiet spot to sit on a Shell A drum. I thought I had done well just hanging on, but Doug Robson expected perfection. Seemed my new best friend didn't suffer amateurs.

Later the pit Marshall called starters for the Star's Sidecar Scratch race. The main sidecar race of the night with the four top riders in a scratch race. Exciting stuff, just the race to the first corner was worth the price of admission.

Doug had a habit of trying to unsettle the other riders by coming slowly into the tapes and doing a bit of grandstanding. There was little love lost between the stars.

When the tapes finally flew, only the lights illuminating the track remained on as the four sidecar teams pushing and shoving roared into the first turn. Again, for me the race was a blur, and despite all of Doug's grandstanding we were last into the first corner. He didn't give up and fought to a hard earned second place. I thought I had done well, but again Doug didn't. I was quick with the goggle changes, a little too quick as it turned out, meaning they were all gone by the second lap which left Doug partly filled in. I had robbed him of another win, and Doug Robson didn't like being beaten by the other stars. It was personal. Back to the Shell A drum in the corner for me.

Our last race was the handicap final. Again, we started from the back mark of 120 yards. This time I didn't put a foot wrong and we crossed the line well in front.

At the end of the meeting Doug loaded the bike and left for home. As always, he didn't stay around for small talk. I thought overall I had done alright, I even signed a couple of autographs outside the pit gate. Teddy and Johnny were impressed and came to the pit gate to congratulate me on my first Showground ride. I was the first to race on the Golden Bowl.

The next day I thought about selling my bike. Now I was riding with Doug Robson it wouldn't be needed. It sure felt good to be a Showground rider at last.

A couple of days later Doug rang.

'Geoff, I don't think you've got what it takes.'

And so ended my very short career as a Speedway Sidecar Passenger.

10

1962

We tied the knot in Rosemary's local church at Rose Bay. My parents were there. It hurt to see them as strangers but they did their best. It was the first time I had seen them together since the breakup.

The reception was at my sister's house at Mascot. A good day with friends and family. Who would be next? Wouldn't be Teddy, he didn't even have a girl at that stage. Maybe Johnny and Carol. Perhaps Harry, he had just met someone special.

We had a one night honeymoon at a motel near Wollongong. I did promise Rosemary we would have a proper honeymoon one day. It would some time in coming.

The new speedway track at nearby Kembla Grange was about to open. Seeing my career as a passenger was well and truly over, I was keen to take a look. So, on the first and only morning of our honeymoon, I took my new bride for a stroll around a dusty speedway track. Then it was time to drive home.

Happily married we settled a nice routine of work family and friends. It wasn't to last. A few weeks later as Rosemary and I arrived home after a night out, we were surprised to see a crowd of people milling outside our house. My sister was there, and Mum, and they were crying. Our lovely old home was no more, gutted by fire, only the walls were left standing. Everything inside was lost, all thanks to a faulty kerosene heater.

The next day Dad came to inspect what was left. I watched as he slowly picked his way through the debris. He didn't talk. Dad had seen the same heartbreaking scene many times in France and Belgium. Now it was our turn.

The house and contents were insured, though no amount of money can compensate for the lifetime of memories. My father seemed so much older that day. The fire and the past few years adding to the damage done.

Ted and John called round to help move my speedway stuff. Fortunately, the workshop was well to the rear of the house and untouched. It was the first time they had met my father and did their best to cheer him up.

The insurance company sent a cheque within a week and work soon commenced on our new house. But there was another problem. Mum had let an adjoining flat. Not a good idea as it turned out as the tenants were uninsured, and threatening to sue. In the meantime, Rosemary and I were fortunate to have a room at my sister's house. Even a place for my speedway bike. By then I was competing regularly at Kembla Grange, and at last chalking up a few wins. Through all this my working life as a parts salesman with Leyland Motors continued to improve though deep down, I still preferred the company of the tannery workers. I missed the lunch time euchre game, the easy banter and I missed Jim. Oh well, at least I no longer smelt like damp leather.

Eventually the new house was finished and we looked forward to resuming normal life. This time with Dad, as Mum had no desire to return to the place of her worst nightmare.

....

The weeks went on and we continued stacking up the wins at Kembla. The track's long straights and tight corners seemed to suit us and we even managed to knock off a few of the Showground's big guns when they ventured down. I began to think maybe, just maybe, we might make it onto the Showground program in the coming season.

One day I saw a newspaper advertisement for a spare parts salesman at Hazell and Moore, the NSW Triumph agents. On a whim I applied. The manager, a Mr. Smith, called me in for an interview. It didn't go well. I explained to Mr. Smith that I knew Triumph motorcycles, and while my spare parts experience was limited to Leyland Motors, parts are parts. Mr. Smith didn't see it that way and politely showed me the door. Turned out he'd done me a favour as a few weeks later a more interesting position was advertised at Tom Byrne Pty. Ltd, the state BMW distributors. I applied in writing and did the interview. A few days later had the job. I didn't bother to ask what the wage was. I didn't care. I was to be part of the motorcycle trade and that was all that mattered.

The manager at Leyland was horrified when I gave notice. How could I give up a career at Leyland for a job in motorcycles? He had almost choked when I said the M word. Of course, he was right, and while I owed my start in the motor trade to Leyland Motors, it was motorbikes I loved. Rosemary was okay with the move, at least I wasn't going back to the tannery.

It is so good to do something that makes you want to get out of bed in the morning. Far better than going through the motions just for money. I couldn't wait to get to work each day. Just walking through the front door at Tom Byrnes was exciting, even though it wasn't all that cool then to work for the BMW distributors. Teddy and Johnny had given me a strange look when I told them about my new job. English bikes were the go in the early sixties. Most other makes were considered daggy. To my friends anyway. And the police used BMWs. How uncool was that? Still, for me any job in the motorcycle business was heaven on a stick. For the first time in my life I looked forward to Monday mornings.

My new boss was Mr. Raymond Whyte. He became my mentor and friend. I was so keen to learn, and learn I did. With the help of Mr. Whyte, I discovered how the motorcycle business worked. More than that, Mr. Whyte taught me about life, ethics and family. My mentor was a fine man. This was life changing stuff for me.

I don't think Mr. Whyte had ever even ridden a motorcycle, and deep down I doubt he even liked them. But had we been selling matchboxes; I am sure he would have approached that with the same enthusiasm.

Mr. Whyte lived in suburban Hurstville with his wife and daughter. Along with his career, they were his main reasons for living. And while Mr. Whyte may not have particularly liked motorcycles, the motorcycle industry liked and respected him. I was indeed fortunate to have such a mentor.

The business was owned by a Mr. Byrne, hence the name Tom Byrne Pty. Ltd. Mr. Byrne travelled into town each afternoon to see how his business was doing, and catch up with the latest gossip. Once settled in his upstairs office he would hold court as one by one his friends and cronies dropped in for a scotch or two. After a few drinks, he would call Mr. Whyte upstairs and then Don Bain the workshop manager would arrive. All the while their voices grew louder as the late afternoon session wore on. Don Bain had been a multiple Australian road racing champion and quite famous in his day. He served with the RAAF in the Second World War. One of the recruits under his command was a young Jack Brabham.

Another famous name at Tom Byrne P/L. was Max Grosskreutz. Max lived in the Sydney harbourside suburb of Rose Bay and had had once been a top international Speedway rider, a household name in both Australia and the U.K. Max was an easygoing unassuming sort of bloke, whenever I could get him to talk about himself, and that wasn't often, I hung on every word. He had grown up on the family cane farm at Proserpine, North Queensland, cutting cane long before he left school. Even as a kid Max mucked around on motorbikes.

One day Max spotted a new 1927 Indian in the window of the town's general store. He had to have it. He was a natural speedway rider even winning the Australian Championship in his second year. Unheard of at the time. That title win secured him a berth with the Australian team, at season's end, he sailed for England.

In those heady days Speedway was huge in the U.K. but the young cane cutter handled the sudden fame and glory with ease. His crowning moment came a few years later, when in front of 84.000 fans, Max captained Australia to an Ashes win at Wembley Stadium. After a long career, including being unlucky not to have won a World Championship, Max finally hung up his leathers and returned home with his new bride. The heat of tropical North Queensland was a little too much for his English Rose and they compromised on Sydney's Eastern Suburbs.

THE GREATEST RACE IN
SPEEDWAY HISTORY
SYDNEY SHOW GROUND Saturday Week
MARCH 2nd

MAX
GROSSKREUTZ
(AUST.)

and

"BLUEY"
WILKINSON
(AUST.)

Who by their daring
and spectacular riding
have brought many
laurels to Australia —
Will meet in a duel that
will surpass any yet
staged.

MAX
GROSSKREUTZ

"BLUEY"
WILKINSON

The skill and endurance displayed in these spectacular contests are the
last "word" in thrills and entertainment.

MONSTER FIREWORKS DISPLAY TO THRILL THE KIDDIES
Save that walk and Park your Car inside the grounds. Ad-
mission : 6 to 7 p.m., 1/-; after 7, 2/-; Children ½ Price. Official
Programmes only inside the Grounds. NO FREE LIST.

EXCITING FROM THE WORD GO !

SEE
THE
WORLD'S
BEST
SPEED-
WAY
RIDERS

Under the direction of
Empire Speedways
1935 Ltd.

SPEED,
SKILL,
THRILLS,
ACTION,
EVERY
SATUR-
DAY
AT
8 P.M.

"THE SPORT WITHOUT AN EQUAL"

As Mr. Whyte showed me around the parts department on my first day, I noticed a few boxes of motorcycle parts that seemed out of place. Curious, I asked what they were. Mr. Whyte didn't appear at all interested and casually explained they were for some new brand, from Japan of all places. They had been handed the N.S.W. distributorship by another company and ordered a few of the 250cc machines to try. Mr. Whyte didn't think they would catch

43

on. The brand's name? YAMAHA.

Over the years, Mr. Whyte had developed a very simple parts system for B.M.W. In no time, I had the hang of things. Then one day when our salesman Sid Seymour was out, I found myself explaining the pros and cons of a new B.M.W. 600 to a prospective buyer. Mr. Whyte winked as I clinched the deal. I was on my way.

There I was in the very small Sydney motorcycle trade. Little did we know a huge change was in the air. The Japanese were coming!

That winter, Harry and I continued to race at Kembla. By then Teddy and Johnny had joined us. Ted on sidecars. John on solos.

One meeting after a week of heavy rain, the track curator covered the soggy surface with fine ash from a local colliery. Harry couldn't ride that weekend and arranged for one of his mates to take his place. A good move as it turned out. The fine ash jammed our carburetor slides wide open and we had a big one. I was unhurt, but not so Harry's replacement who broke both collarbones. Teddy did much the same thing in the next race, fortunately, only hurting he and his passenger's dignity.

It was a long drive home with Rosemary lecturing me on the number of accidents I had already suffered in my very short career. I assured her, with the laws of average, my luck had to change. 'We'll see,' she said unconvinced. 'In the meantime, I christen thee, Autumn Leaves.'

Come September we lined up for the pre-season Showground practice day. Our one chance to show the promotion we were ready for the big time.

What a difference to Kembla Grange. The showground track was narrow and super-fast. The older well-established riders knew it like the back of their hands.

Doug gave me a few pointers and out we went. Though I did have the one night's experience riding passenger, holding the handlebars was another thing altogether. We gave it our best shot, but after the three laps allocated, I knew we were not yet quite quick enough. Same for John and Ted.

Ever the optimist, I rang the showground promoter Mr. Sherwood the following Monday. 'Can't use you at the moment Geoff,' he simply said and promptly hung up. From then on, my weekly torment was to pluck up the courage to ring Mr. Sherwood and cope with rejection.

One Monday, after a big meeting at Kembla, I cheekily told Mr. Sherwood Harry and I had trounced a couple of his stars who had made a rare appearance on the tricky South Coast track. Mr. Sherwood was a man of few words, 'I'll see what I can do for you Geoff.' He added something I couldn't quite hear, but before I dared to ask the great man to repeat himself, he had hung up. Oh well I thought, one day. Mr. Whyte overheard the conversation. 'I'll give you this Geoffrey Grocott,' he said smiling. 'You are one persistent fellow.' Persistent, or a pain? I guess I was a bit of both. Anyway, the Triumph needed some engine work, and as Kembla was held fortnightly I decided to pull the motor apart for a quick overhaul.

The next Saturday night Rosemary and I arrived at the showground, early as usual to be sure of a good seat. Once settled in the stand, I flicked through the program and did a double take. Listed in the encourage sidecar handicap was one Geoff Grocott and Harry Ross. Stunned, I showed the program to Rosemary. 'That'll be the end of me with Mr. Sherwood,' I groaned. 'And after all my pestering.'

Rosemary wasn't fazed, 'Why don't you ask Doug for a lend of his bike?' 'Doug Robson?' I replied. 'I wouldn't dare. Anyway, I've never ridden a Vincent.'

Rosemary shook her head, 'No, not Doug Robson. Doug Tyreman, his bikes not all that different to yours.'

Doug Tyreman was a hot Showground sidecar racer, the only Triumph rider who at times could compete with the big Vincents. We were sort of friends, though he and Harry were closer. Maybe he'd do it for Harry.

Ever confident, Rosemary was soon on her way to our nearby home to collect my leathers while I hurried to the pits to beg Doug Tyreman. My showground future was in his hands. I found him and Harry outside the pits. Harry had beaten me to it.

Doug was happy to help, and fortunately Harry had his leathers in his car's boot. A little dirty, but that was a minor thing.

Rosemary battled the crowds on her way back just arriving in the nick of time. I dashed to the change rooms and quickly changed into my leathers.

Then the nerves set in. A few minutes later I heard the pit marshal call my name. This was it.

The pit gates slowly opened and Doug wheeled his bike out under the bright lights. I could just hear the track announcer saying something about a new young rider, one Geoff Grocott.

Doug bump started the bike and passed me the handlebars. I needed a pee, badly. It may have only been the lowly sidecar encourage event, but it was my one big chance.

On the way to the starting line I kept repeating to myself, Win this and you're on your way. Win this and you're on your way.

As we came into the starting line I looked up to the stand where Rosemary was and nodded. Suddenly the red lights went out and I held my breath for the whole three laps. Finally, after what seemed a lifetime, the checkered flag. We had won.

On the way back to the pits Harry patted my leg and I happily patted him back. There would be no more nervous Monday morning phone calls to Mr. Sherwood. But I still called him mister.

The following week we were on the program proper, starting from the lowly handicap mark of zero.

As the season progressed, we slowly improved our handicap status. By the season's end we had chalked up a respectable number of wins. Harry and I also continued competing at Kembla. Though it was small time compared to the Showground, Kembla was a rider's track, I needed all the experience I could get.

Geoff and Harry. Early days at the Showground.

Teddy made it onto the Showground program later that season. Johnny had to wait a while. Teddy and I tried to convince him to try his luck on sidecars, but John was determined to do his own thing. I thought John too big for a Solo, as most of the top riders were thin and wiry. He was going nowhere, but I was sure he would make one hell of a sidecar rider. Anyway, I had enough problems of my own just trying to keep up with the Vincent riders. I knew I had to have one for myself. All season I had saved my prize money, and Mum said she would help. I scouted around for a suitable bike.

I heard a rumour there was a Vincent road bike for sale, in of all places, just around the corner from our home. The young owner was reluctant to part with his much-loved machine, but he needed the money. I rode home on a magnificent 1000cc Vincent Rapide and we wasted no time in converting it to a full-blown speedway sidecar. The very latest Amal GP carburetors, high compression pistons, straight through exhausts and methanol fuel. When the modified Vincent was fired up for the first time, our driveway shook.

With our first child, due in May, and Rosemary not at all well, we were fortunate to have a wonderful doctor living and practicing in our very own street. She was to help Rosemary through an extremely difficult pregnancy. Nothing was too much trouble for our beloved doctor who treated her patients on a need first, ability to pay second. That wonderful human was

47

one of Adolph's rejects. Thanks for that, Adolph.

The autumn of 1962 was one of Sydney's wettest. An asthmatic's nightmare. Before long hospitals wards were full to brimming, and before long, I too was in the Asthma Ward at the Prince Henry Hospital on Sydney's beautiful southern coastline. Ventolin wasn't around then; the usual treatment was adrenaline injections or tablets. After a week I was sent home, but by the next morning I was again gasping for breath. Heavily pregnant Rosemary ran for the doctor who stabilised me and called the hospital. I overheard her say, 'If he dies, it would be on their hands.'

Back in the Asthma ward with my arms like pincushions and my hair falling out, Teddy and Johnny came to visit. In their usual way they made light of things. They even convinced the nurse to allow them to watch her jab me with my two-hourly needle. By then Rosemary was some eight months pregnant. She put on a brave face as she watched me slowly deteriorate.

There was one intern who seemed to be at the hospital twenty-four hours a day. Some of the patients had christened him "Doctor Wheezencough". For me he seemed the only medico truly interested in our getting out of there alive. I was then in my third week, and going downhill fast. When I mentioned this to one of the immaculately dressed Macquarie Street specialists, he simply barked, 'If you continue to think like that, you will never recover.'

Every morning Dr. Wheezencough called by on his rounds. One day he asked if I was interested in trying a new medication. At that stage I was prepared to try anything, I didn't think my ticker could take much more. He explained it was a device that dispensed a drug called Ventolin that you inhaled through a Puffer. He didn't know if it would help, but would appreciate my giving it a try. A few days later I was on my way home with my new best friend "Puffer" safely in my pocket. The next week I was back racing and in May our daughter was born.

We called our new arrival Linda, and what a wonderful change she made to all our lives. Johnny was over the moon; family was everything to him. And then he and Carol tied the knot, even Ted the confirmed bachelor was in love. But again, our bliss was not to last. The tenants who'd rented my mother's backyard flat sued and we lost the case. The Mascot house was to be sold to cover costs; the balance left to be used for the purchase of a cheaper house in Western Sydney. Rosemary and I didn't want to leave the

Mascot area and looked around for something to rent. In the end, we went with Dad.

Johnny 1963

Geoff and Teddy 1964

11

1963   Granville-Western Sydney

The new house was a triple fronted fibro cottage on an unsealed street in Granville-Western Sydney. We hated it from day one.

I bought a small road bike to do battle with the Parramatta Road traffic, while Rosemary adapted to her new life. As luck would have it, Maureen, who lived opposite, had a daughter around Linda's age. They hit it off. Maureen told us she had grown up on Scotland Island and I remember asking why she didn't have an accent. Maureen just laughed explaining that Scotland Island was actually in Pittwater on the northern beaches of Sydney. Her parents had recently traded the family house for a cruising yacht and headed off on a world cruise. Maureen had stayed behind with her new husband and like us bought a cheap house in Western Sydney. That day, as we stood and chatted on our hot dusty dirt road, Scotland Island sounded

50

like a paradise, though perhaps no place for a budding speedway rider and his Vincent.

Living in Western Sydney wasn't all bad, Teddy and his new wife Lyn, and his mum, lived nearby. At least we were again close to each other. As housing commission tenants, they'd had little choice when the department moved them, though I suspect Ted's mum was happy just to have a roof over their heads. I never heard her complain. Then again, she wasn't the complaining type. Nor was Ted.

I had another friend who lived nearby. Peter White, a high school student I had first met at Doug Robson's place. Peter was very much the quiet dedicated speedway fan who lived and breathed the sport. Much later he would publish his own speedway magazine, "Peter White's Speedway World"

Living in the west, meant we were closer to the road race and short circuit tracks. When I wasn't riding, we would often head off to enjoy watching others compete for a change.

Dad seemed indifferent with the move. Retired, he spent his much of his spare time repairing the house or watching over his new granddaughter. In the meantime, I converted an old chicken coop at the rear of the yard into my workshop. It was ordinary, but at least it didn't leak. I cannot remember one time my father even so much as looked at my Vincent. It was simply my folly.

Before we left Mascot, I had reluctantly sold my faithful Triumph. With the new Vincent ready, my original faithful steed was redundant. A buyer appeared in the most unusual circumstance.

Two good looking young blokes, Gary Innis and Reggie Proctor, managed the Mascot butchery where Rosemary sometime did her shopping. Their specialty wasn't sausages though, more flirting with the many Yummy Mummies who called into their shop. Rosemary too was one their Yummy Mummies. What she didn't know was the two young Romeos were passionate speedway followers, and like me a year or so before were desperate to find a way in. Come the first practice day at the Showground they were, as usual, hanging around the pit gate watching their favourite riders arrive. When Rosemary and I turned up with our new Vincent, Gary Innis later told me how they were gob smacked to discover one of their favourite Yummy Mummies was married to a Speedway Sidecar Rider. Next time Rosemary called into their shop, the lads stopped serving and pounced.

'Are you Geoff Grocott's wife? they chorused. 'Would you introduce us?'

So, Gary and Reg bought my faithful Triumph and a few weeks later they began their speedway apprenticeship at Kembla Grange. In time, Gary would become my soul mate and closest friend.

Before long we met Carmel, Gary's pretty young wife. Carmel was a country girl, and a nurse at a Sydney hospital. She'd had no idea of his racing ambitions, but like Rosemary reluctantly went along with the speedway thing hoping he would soon tire of it.

Aboard the Vincent, Harry and I rapidly improved our handicap rating and finished the season on 90 yards behind. Just short of A grade.

Half way through, we had yet another big one. Hit the fence hard and flew high in the air. I broke my collarbone while Harry simply dusted himself off and rode in the next race with Doug Tyerman. Harry Ross was one tough cookie. Fortunately, it was my left collarbone meaning I could still do most of my tasks at work. Anyway, it wasn't a problem at Tom Byrne P/L. They were happy to have a budding speedway rider behind the counter. The odd accident and a little time off were all part of the deal.

After a few weeks recuperating we were back into it. By then Teddy too was on a Vincent, and going well.

A Villawood newspaper ran a story on Teddy. The sort of local kid going places thing. His mum was proud. Not only was her son a good bloke, he was somebody. In one of my favourite books, "The Catcher in the Rye", Holden Caulfield speaks glowingly of his long dead younger brother who had died of Leukemia. When I read that passage, I immediately thought of Teddy, it could have been him the author described.

There weren't many sporting stars in the new Villawood Housing Estate so Teddy had lots of young admirers, particularly John who lived a few doors down. John had Cerebral Palsy. Many then thought sufferers a little simple but Teddy knew different. John was an intelligent young man. They became close friends.

But no matter how tough times were on the streets of the Villawood Housing Estate, it was still the era of unlocked doors and safe streets. Same at nearby Granville, though we did have our Holden stolen from our driveway one night. The police found it a couple of days later unharmed.

At the end of the season Harry decided to call it quits. He had recently married, and was fast losing interest. I was sorry to see him go as we'd had good times together. Meanwhile, my young friend Peter White had begun to ride passenger after scoring a ride with Col Denny, another ex-passenger turned rider. And there I thought it would end. Peter just didn't seem the type. He was a bank clerk, an occupation that seemed to suit him. I figured he would go on to become a mild-mannered accountant and settle down with a couple of kids. Little did I know, there was another side to the skinny kid from Sefton. Peter kept on with Col, and went okay, and no one was more surprised than me. When he asked to replace Harry on the Vincent, I gave it a lot of thought. After checking with his parents, he was on. I think Peter's main reason in riding passenger was more the girls he intended to impress. It sure turned out that way.

We went on to have a couple of good seasons together with never a dull moment. The mild-mannered bank teller was an iron man. No pre-race nerves for Peter, always as cool as Willy the Penguin. While I usually had a touch of the butterflies before the first race, Peter would wander around the pits munching on a hot dog. At times, he would go missing but our pit crew always knew where to find him. Outside the pit gate chatting to some girl.

The big test for a speedway sidecar passenger was to hold his nerve when another rider gave him a serve. Namely a whack in the back with the sidecar wheel. Peter passed that test many times, and carried the tyre marks on the back of his leathers to prove it. One night he turned up with a pair of white boots, but no amount of pleading would make me do the same. I still hadn't forgotten the Bopper and the silver boots episode.

At the end of our second season we tied for the season's handicap point score. It was to be decided the next week with a run off against Jude Sanderson and his passenger the young Warren Sullivan. That was the first time I had seen Peter nervous, he so badly wanted to win. Would be another feather in his cap with the girls. Unfortunately, I missed a gear and blew it, though later that night we had our first win in the Stars Sidecar Scratch. That helped soften Peter's disappointment.

Meanwhile the motorcycle world was fast changing as the Japanese bikes began to sell in ever increasing numbers. Came the month when Yamaha outsold BMW and after his earlier prediction that Japanese motorcycles would never be more than a novelty, Mr. Whyte gladly ate humble pie. The small motorcycle business was on the up and up. We even sold new motorbikes to women.

One day an American cattleman from the Northern Territory came in to order a couple of new Yamahas. I recognised him from an article I'd read. He was Mr. Randolph Galt, once married to the Hollywood actress Anne Baxter. For a time, she lived on his huge remote cattle station deep in the outback. The marriage eventually failed and she returned to America later penning a book, "Intermission- a True Story". In it she bagged Australia, her hick neighbours, and the boring life she'd endured here. From what I saw of the tall, good looking and unassuming Mr. Galt that morning, I would say Miss Baxter was the loser. Later we delivered his bikes with the changes he had requested. It seemed Mr. Galt knew far more about motorbikes than women as the Yamahas he designed were forerunners to the Japanese agricultural models that changed farming practices.

Around this time, Barry Ryan of Ryan's motorcycles at Parramatta, quietly offered me a position with his firm. It was very tempting. More money, close to home, plus the prestige of being involved as most of his staff were well known motorcycle racers. In the end, I just couldn't do it. Mr. Whyte and Mr. Byrne had given me a start in the motorcycle industry. I owed them; I couldn't let them down.

One day, we staff were asked to stay back for a special motorcycle showing. Probably a new Yamaha model I thought. But when the cover was removed, there stood an entirely new marque with a badge previously unknown to me. Kawasaki. I was very much a Yamaha man, not at all interested in another brand from Japan, though I had to admit the 350cc model was very advanced for the times. Its twin rotary disc valve engine was then only seen on Grand Prix bikes, and the overall finish was very good. I gathered Mr. Byrne was hedging his bets, perhaps concerned the time may come when a new and larger company would be handed the Yamaha distributorship. All too soon he would be proved correct.

Though Yamaha sales were booming, it was BMW motorcycles that had always served Tom Byrne well. All through the bad times, the exclusive agency had kept the doors open when so many failed. The distributorship also meant a rather lucrative trade in spare parts with many customers making the comment that Mr. Byrne was more than a little enthusiastic with his mark ups. The part's prices did seem rather high, but I was told from day

54

one to counter any complaints with, 'In the long run they're cheaper because you use less.' BMW then was an enthusiast's only motorcycle with a small hardcore following of mainly touring motorcyclists and European migrants.

One afternoon as I was about to leave for the day, Mr. Byrne in his usual gruff voice called out, 'Geoffrey, pop up before you go if you don't mind.'

I didn't mind, maybe I was about to get a promotion or something. A pay rise would have been nice. Deep down I was still kicking myself for knocking back the Ryan's Motorcycle's offer.

Upstairs Mr. Byrne was entertaining the usual bunch of cronies sipping their scotch and ice.

'Care for a stimulant Geoffrey?'

That was Mr. Byrne's way of asking if I'd like a drink. I didn't. I never really developed a taste for the stuff until much later.

'Good boy. Now, I need you to do a spot of spying for me.'

Spying? There went the pay rise. Anyway, what would I know about spying? He went on, 'There's a chap illegally selling BMW parts. Lives near you. Name's Galvin. Know him?'

It was news to me but was it illegal to sell motorcycle parts? As far as Mr. Byrne was concerned it was, especially if they were BMW parts. The cronies heartily agreed as they knocked back another of his best scotch.

Reluctantly I agreed to check out this Galvin bloke. Seemed I was to be an industrial spy, but still no hint of a pay rise.

The Galvin house was only a few streets from ours, for a while I rode past each morning to check the scene. Didn't seem to be much happening, no signs, just another ordinary triple fronted fibro place like ours.

A week later I reported back to Mr. Byrne and informed him I couldn't see anything at the Galvin house that indicated a BMW parts business. Mr. Byrne was not happy.

Turned out I had failed badly at my first spying attempt. John Galvin was indeed running a thriving parts business, and growing by the day, though his prices weren't. Much later, Mr. Byrne and John Galvin would kiss and makeup and John would go on to be a leading figure in the motorcycle industry. Later John and I would become close friends. When I confessed to my spying, he forgave me with a laugh adding he had often wondered about the dork on the little Yamaha who for a while rode slowly past his house each morning.

Geoff and Peter on the Vincent 1964

Doug Robson, Rob Lewis, Johnny O'keefe & his son

Doug with Aussie rock star J.O.K.

56

Geoff and Peter with the Vincent.
Showground Pits 1964.

12

1964

Ever so slowly we adapted to Western Sydney life. Dad seemed content at last, he and Rosemary had bonded as father and daughter.

Before long the dusty street was sealed, and fortunately our neighbours didn't seem to mind my bump starting the big Vincent down the driveway on Saturday afternoons. Most thought it cool to have a rising young speedway rider in their street.

At times, I had to ask Rosemary to jump in the sidecar if I needed to start it for some reason or other. When a highly tuned 1000cc Vincent fires up, the sidecar isn't exactly the right place for a lady, but after the usual protests she handled it well. I've always used the, "Jump into the sidecar" thing as a measure of my ideal woman. Fortunately, I had married one who would do just that.

After a while Dad began attending weekly dances at nearby Strathfield. It was good to see him at last out and about. By then Dad and Teddy were good friends. Ted was the only person I heard my father speak of the events that led to his Distinguished Conduct Medal. Dad simply finished the conversation with, 'It was a silly thing to do.' Many years later I would learn he had only revealed part of the story. So much happened on that day in France.

I envied Teddy's easy going relationship with my father, something I just couldn't seem to achieve. So many things were left unsaid between us, then again, Teddy rarely talked of his own father, very much his mother's son.

As our little daughter Linda grew and developed her own personality, Dad would often read to her from Little Golden Books. For hours on end they would read together. Eventually Linda learned all the stories by heart and would pretend to read along with her grandfather. I loved to watch the quiet gentle man with his granddaughter.

One day, when I was around five or six, I overheard an adult conversation at our Sydney Maroubra house. For a long time after, I was a little afraid of my father. As usual, I'd hidden under my bed when the friends arrived. Later, after Mum promised me a cake or something, I came out. They were talking about war and I was woofing cake. Dad wasn't there. Mum said something like, 'Hands up-hands down. Fred shot them all.' The visitors seemed quite pleased with this. I guess in the late forties few tears were shed for dead Germans. People then were only beginning to recover from the second lot, for them there was no such thing as a "Good German". Mum went on to describe the scene after my father had finished. It wasn't pretty.

When Dad came home, I thought about what she'd said. I had never heard my father so much as raise his voice. I was confused. And years later, there he was, a quiet gentle older man patiently reading the same stories over and over to his granddaughter. Whatever it was that the young shearer from Murrumbateman had done long ago was buried somewhere in the past. Or was it?

13
1965-1966

All that long winter, Teddy and I worked hard on our Vincents determined to finally make A grade in the coming season. Meanwhile John persevered with his J.A.P. Solo. No argument from us could convince him to make the switch to Sidecars.

To make a few extra quid I worked some months cleaning offices. Starting at five before rushing off to my day job at nine. It was hard going, but I needed the money as Rosemary was expecting again.

Another hard pregnancy followed with Rosemary spending the final month alone in a darkened room at Auburn District Hospital. My father watched on with knowing eyes. He'd been down the same road. My mother had almost died when I came into the world. I was their last.

Rosemary and Linda missed each other dreadfully as no contact with children was allowed. Dad and I could only take Linda as far as the grounds for Rosemary to sneak onto a balcony and wave. Then the tears would flow. Finally, mother and new baby daughter Carol were home and all was good.

Teddy was besotted with little Carol. There seemed a special bond between them. Teddy was so good with kids, not one mean bone in his big body. Every time he came around, Carol and Linda were over the moon. No one played hide and seek like their big cuddly Teddy Bear uncle.

When the summer speedway season began, it seemed all of Teddy's hard work was paying off. His rating at the Showground improved week after week. Before long he was giving me a start in handicap races. Then he made A grade.

At times I thought perhaps Teddy was taking it all a little too seriously, or maybe I was a little envious of his success. He began to carry a small rubber ball everywhere. 'It's to strengthen my right wrist that has been giving me a few problems,' he said. Though to watch him ride with the throttle hard against the stop, one would never know. One day as we talked about a modification he'd made to his Vincent, not once did he let up on that ball. Something in his eyes made me a little uneasy. My best friend was so determined to reach the top.

5th. FEBRUARY 1966.

It was a simple accident. I was watching from the pits as I hadn't qualified for the handicap final, the last bike race of the night.

Ted was in great form that night, he rocketed down the starting straight towards the first corner. Suddenly a front marker fumbled a gear change. The passenger raised a warning arm and the field thundered past. But Teddy's view had been obscured until the last moment. He clipped the slowed bike and overturned. I wasn't alarmed. They weren't at full speed. We had both walked away from much worse.

I went to the change rooms to get out of my leathers, thinking I'd give him a stir up later. Maurie Ford, one of the senior riders, came and spoke to me.

'You had better go to the Hospital Geoff. He's pretty bad.'

I wondered who Maurie was talking about.

'Who is?'

Maurie gently placed his hand on my shoulder, 'Sorry mate, I thought you knew.'

The heavy Vincent had landed on Teddy causing massive head injuries. His passenger Charles Green was unhurt.

As the Ambos worked on Teddy, a hush came over the crowd. They could sense something was seriously wrong. All the while I was in the change room unaware of what was happening.

I rushed from the pits to find Rosemary waiting. Little was said as we hurried to the hospital.

Before long, a large group of competitors and supporters were gathered outside St. Vincent's Hospital anxiously awaiting some news. When it finally came, it was all bad. We stood stunned, not quite knowing what to do.

After a while, I don't remember how long, Teddy's mother arrived by taxi. To this day, I can still see the lost look in her eyes as she made her way through the crowd. When she saw John and I, she knew everyone was there for her son. Mrs. Preston feared the worst. By the time she made his bedside it was all over.

A little later, someone from the hospital informed the crowd and we slowly wandered off. Rosemary and I didn't speak on the long drive home.

Fortunately, the girls had stayed home with their grandfather that night and were fast asleep when we arrived. We left it at that. There'd be time enough in the morning.

In a daze the next morning I absently went through the motions. Unload Vincent, remove trailer, take leathers from car boot. Wash leathers, wash Vincent, the Showground dirt stuck like glue. I retreated to my workshop come chicken coop. I had a need to be alone.

In the house the children played as usual. Too young to know. Dad was quiet as he too had lost a friend. Another on his long list.

Later Rosemary came up to tell me someone wanted to see me. I wasn't in the mood. She said it was important.

Nervously waiting at the door were the riders involved in Teddy's accident, Mick and John Pearson. Guilt showed on their faces.

Rosemary brought us a cup of tea and we talked quietly for a while. I said for them to not even think of retiring. That was the last thing Teddy would have wanted. It was simply a missed gear change. Just one of those things.

In time, the Pearson brothers and I would become close friends but unfortunately it would cause a deep irreparable rift between Johnny and me.

At work Mr. Whyte tried to comfort me, 'Geoff. Teddy knew what he was doing. He wouldn't want you to go to pieces.' But even my mentor couldn't console me, such was my grief.

The night before the funeral I dreamed Teddy was back. I told him he had us so worried but Teddy just smiled and said, 'Ge-off, you knew I'd come back.'

I awoke suddenly. It was all a dream. Even after all these years, should somebody call me Ge-off, a shiver runs down my spine.

The funeral at Rookwood cemetery was a huge affair. Seemed everyone from Australian Speedway and the British Motor Corporation were there. Ted's mum looked so lost, so fragile. We exchanged a glance but I could only manage a knowing nod. There was nothing I could find to say. My mother had once said, 'In the war years, one could see death in the eyes of the mothers who had lost a son.' And so it would be with Teddy's mum.

John, Teddy's young friend from the housing estate, was there, alone, crutches by his side. I wondered what he would do without his best friend. I supposed Ted's father was there, somewhere, too many people to know.

Later we went back to Lyn's parent's house for a sort of wake. John was upset and angry. 'It was all the fault of those Pearson bastards,' he spat out. I tried to reason, but John was having none of it. His best mate was dead and they were to blame. I argued Ted wouldn't have wanted that. He knew the dangers. But John just glared. The Pearson brothers had made themselves an enemy. All I could hope was time would soften John's bitterness. I didn't dare tell him they had called at my home. John expected his friends to be loyal, just my talking to them had broken his code.

A few days later I rang Mr. Sherwood. After all the begging calls, I asked to be taken off the program. My heart was no longer in it.

Life went on. Most days I rode past the cemetery on my way to work. I could have taken a different route, but somehow it was comforting to be close to Teddy, if only for the moment.

The day after the funeral I visited Ted's gravesite alone. Different without the crowds. His resting place was in a new lawn section surrounded by beautiful trees and gardens. I noticed the plot next to Teddy was empty, a few weeks later I found myself at the cemetery office enquiring if it was for sale. I didn't know why I bought it, perhaps it was part of my grieving. Later, Lyn had a plaque and picture placed on Teddy's headstone. I often visited to sit on the adjoining stone wall and think. I had just turned twenty four, but the thought of impending death was always with me. At least I knew where I would be when it happened.

Buying the grave hadn't improved things with Johnny. When he discovered what I had done he exploded once more. Something about me not letting go. John didn't visit the cemetery, wasn't his thing. And nothing had softened his anger towards the Pearson brothers.

I continued going to the speedway on Saturday nights, only as a spectator. It was hard to break old habits as most of our friends were involved in speedway one way or another.

Later that year I sold my beloved Vincent speedway outfit to close friend Gary Innis. Gary had bought my Triumph, then my Vincent. My speedway days were well and truly finished. At least my bike went to a good home.

14

BURRENDONG

A few months after Teddy's death, Mum asked me to take her to childhood home for a final goodbye. The valley she grew up in was about to disappear under the waters of the Burrendong Dam. We thought it a good chance to escape Sydney for a while. Lyn Preston would come along as well, anything to take her mind off Teddy.

When Johnny heard of the trip, he insisted we take his brand-new car. Perhaps it was a peace gesture, one could only hope.

John had just purchased a brand new black Valiant S model. very flash at the time. But the car meant more than just being flash for John, more a symbol of his new place in the world. No longer was he the kid from a rundown rented house in Newtown. John was married and saving for a house, and about to buy a truck to go into business for himself. I still lived in hope one day we'd be back together. Fishing in the bay. Mucking around with our dogs. Spending good time like the old days. I hated my falling out with Johnny. With Teddy gone, he should have been my closest and dearest friend. At times, I wondered if I should have simply avoided the Pearson brothers and stayed loyal to Johnny. When old friends fall out, they fall hard.

We gratefully accepted John's offer of the car. As he handed me the keys, I thought, maybe, just maybe, our war was over.

The next morning, six of us, Mum, Rosemary, Lyn, her sister, and our kids, headed west for the long drive to Wellington in the central west of NSW.

We stayed the night in a motel and first thing set out to drive the thirty or so kilometres to the Burrendong Valley. To begin the road was bitumen, then came the dirt. We travelled for miles as it narrowed to what was little more than a rough track. Every now and then we'd come to a closed gate. Mum would jump out, open the gate and wave us through. Didn't seem to be any stock around, just the odd rabbit, but Mum being a country girl carefully closed every gate behind us.

Occasionally we passed the foundations of a demolished homestead with only the chimneys left standing, the rest moved to who knew where. Once loved gardens lay dying. Fruit trees already beginning to grow wild. Didn't matter, they had little time left.

We stopped at an old gnarled tree to pick quinces for Dad. He'd learned to make good quince pies from a shearer's cook. At least there'd be something to take back. We picked wild apricots and peaches, and listened to the silence. The valley was eerily quiet that morning, almost as if the birds and animals knew what was coming. Even most of the dreaded rabbits were gone. The damage done no longer of any consequence.

During the eighteen hundreds the rabbit arrived and thrived in the fertile valley. Before long they were in plague proportions. From then on it was it a constant battle between man and rabbit. Though many made a living trapping for the skins, total eradication was always the number one priority. For a time, it seemed man had won, but when the young men were again away in another world war, once more the rabbit ran wild. In those few short years the beautiful land and river banks were devastated. When the war between humans came to an end, war with the rabbit resumed.

In the early years of white settlement, the valley was prime merino country. Local aborigines and pastoralists got on well. The tribes had always lived with their own code of conduct, and while they had the odd battle, in the main they cohabited happily on either side of the river. Then gold was discovered and miners came, with them a town, streets, shops, hotels and wine shanties. For a time, the Burrendong village supported over a thousand people. Then the Chinese arrived, lots of them. They were good at the gold thing. Some didn't like that.

More miners came. Forty-Niners from the California fields. Hard men who had butchered American Indians. Shoot first, ask questions later. And they brought their diseases. In a few short years, the natives that were left quietly drifted away. No sign of any of this now. Once the easy pickings were over, most left for another gold rush in another place. My family, the Newtons and Edens, stayed on. Some to work the land, others to continue with the gold.

So many questions I should have asked that day, but I was too young to fully appreciate my family's history in that soon to be lost valley. Fortunately, others have recorded some of it. Mum always believed she knew where undiscovered gold lay hidden in her valley. She intended to return one day; I was to come along. Too late for any of that now, any undiscovered gold would soon be under the water. Perhaps the best place for it.

For what seemed miles, we drove alongside a fast running creek. I couldn't see where, or how, to cross, and I sure didn't want to hurt Johnnie's new car. Mum wasn't worried, she knew where the crossing was.

Finally Mum pointed, I hoped she knew what she was doing, and Mum did. We made it safely to the other side with the Valliant's wheels glistening from their fresh water wash.

Then we were at her old school by the Mudgee River. For some reason the tiny schoolhouse had been left pretty much complete. The Newtons were illiterate when they came to the valley. I have seen a copy of a document my great grandfather could only sign with an X. Later one of his children became a teacher. The power of education.

We drove from the school to Mum's old house, or where it once stood. She said it wasn't far as she'd walked to school every day. But it was far.

Mum loved the valley. Lots of friends and relatives were close by. But they couldn't help when the creek was up, as it always seemed to be when one of the children were sick, and her father again away shearing.

We came to what was left of her house. Again, old fruit trees marked the place. Mum walked quietly through the remnants. We left her alone to say her goodbyes.

My mother was happiest when her father was home from shearing. An easy going dad she loved dearly. But life in the valley could be hard and cruel with small children the most vulnerable. Of her nine siblings, only two would survive childhood. Mum's recurring nightmare is attempting to cross the flooded creek, her mother hysterical with another sick child.

Eventually her mother could take no more. She left the valley with her two surviving children. Her husband, James Newton my grandfather, stayed behind. They never saw each other again.

From all accounts, my grandmother, Edith May Newton nee Eden, was a highly intelligent woman. An animal lover and vegetarian, unusual for the times. In later years, she turned to her church and lived out her days with

67

family in Lithgow.

There are no headstones in the valley. No place to lay flowers. Mum stood among the old fruit trees where most were buried. Two of her sisters, born ten years apart, and both christened Edith May, are in a small nearby cemetery.

In 1890, Frederick Mc. Cubbin painted the haunting, A Bush Grave, that captured the grief and helplessness of a pioneer family as they buried yet another child.

Back in the car my mother's thoughts were with her long lost brothers and sisters. After a while she said softly, 'I thought they should have been moved into town before the rains came. But perhaps it's for the best, now they'll always be part of the valley.'

My mother cried for weeks after they left Burrendong. For her father, her milking cow, her friends and relatives. Eventually she did adapt to life in Sydney, though she always remained a country girl at heart.

I don't know how or where my parents met. Dad had moved to Sydney after his first marriage ended, something never discussed in front of us kids. I was told there were no children, save for his bride's younger sister who they raised as their own. He had married Gladys McKeig at St Thomas Church in North Sydney some six weeks after returning from the First World War. I guess she was his childhood sweetheart. They returned to Yass where he built a lovely home for them, but the marriage ended after some fifteen years.

I did discover my father had once owned a motorcycle and sidecar, though he never once mentioned it to me. Perhaps it involved his first wife and bad memories. I'd like to think that was the only reason we never talked sidecars.

All these years later I wonder about the younger sister. Was she really a sister, or did Dad and Gladys have an affair just before he left for the front? In those days, an unwanted pregnancy was often passed off as a late arrival. Did they come up with the story in case my father didn't return and when he came back was it too late to change the story? Was that little girl my half-sister? I guess I'll never really know, though I do have a feeling there was another sister out there somewhere.

For my mother, the young waitress in the small village of Penrith west of Sydney, the good-looking war hero would have been quite a catch. Though he was some sixteen years older, they fell in love and made a handsome couple as they walked down the aisle of the Penrith Methodist church in April 1936.

My mother's childhood experiences left her with little time for fools or whiners. No room for Prima Donnas in our family. Nor bullshit artists. But there was once music in our home. Laughter and books, lots of books. We listened to the radio, we had fun, we did things together. I thought we were the perfect family. Then she left.

Back in Sydney all seemed well with Johnny, until he heard I had helped the Pearson brothers with their Vincent. We had another blazing row. Johnny accused me of betraying Teddy's memory, and went on and on about the cemetery plot. We were back to square one. This time I didn't argue, though I was deeply hurt. Our once deep close friendship seemed damaged beyond repair, and I blamed myself.

Life went on.

The long daily commute to the city in heavy traffic was beginning to get me down, I began to think of a way out. The thought of my own business close to home had crossed my mind once or twice, though I dismissed it as another of my dreams. It hadn't been all that long since I was let out of the tannery, the idea of my being self employed seemed another world. My parents had their own mixed business for a while, soon after they married. The shop wasn't a success. For a time, Mum had run it on her own while Dad returned to shearing. There was some problem with a tenant who lived in the flat above and that hadn't helped matters. Apparently, there was no way to evict him, or have him pay a reasonable rent. Mother blamed the Labor Party for that, and for anything else that went wrong. From then on she was a loyal Liberal supporter, though even that was up for change depending on her mood, and who was the prime minister at the time. In the end, the business was all too hard and they sold at a loss. Back in Yass us kids got in the way, and that was that. Still, the business thing gave me something to think about on my long ride home.

At times, I would stop and spend time with Teddy. Sit quietly on the stone wall and think. His section of the cemetery was filling fast. I was glad I bought the plot, no matter what John thought. By then my grief had changed to a dull sorrow, and while I had finally come to terms with Ted's passing, a feeling of impending doom still haunted me.

69

15
1967

When the Showground promotion reintroduced the British vs. Australia Solo Tests, Speedway once more boomed in Australia. The first match in Sydney drew an official crowd of 35,000, and was a tad conservative, as long before the meeting got under way the gates were closed. Even the stairways in the stands were full of eager fans. The tests were a great success and it seemed then the Sydney Showground Speedway would go forever.

While I had no thoughts of returning to sidecars, I'd heard on the grapevine that Johnny Dunne was about to do just that. And on Teddy's Vincent. The bike hadn't been touched since the fatal accident, not that it had suffered much damage. John Hall, a mutual friend and top mechanic, was to prepare it for John's debut. I wasn't included in the arrangements, nor did I expect to be as Johnny and I rarely spoke to each other. Silently I wished them well. But I had other things on my mind when Rosemary was diagnosed with cancer. Again, we were fortunate to have a good doctor in our local G.P Dr. Darroch. He was a knock about sort of medico, ex-Navy, and not all that fussed with bedside manner. Every time Rosemary and baby daughter Carol attended his clinic he pressured her to take the tests. Rosemary thought at twenty-five she was too young to worry about such things and resisted. Finally, she did what she was told and when the results came back there was no doubt. Cervical cancer. Another long period at Auburn Hospital followed. There would be no more children.

Eventually Rosemary was home and our life slowly returned to normal. By then I had made up my mind to have a go at a motorcycle franchise. Mum was happy to lend a few bob, actually, a little more than that, and Mr. Whyte gave me his blessings. All I had to do was find suitable premises around Yagoona in south west Sydney. The area was close to home with no other motorcycle dealer for miles. By then Tom Byrne had lost the Yamaha franchise, fortunately he'd had the foresight in securing the Kawasaki distributorship. The Sydney motorcycle industry was quite insular in those days, meaning the new Yamaha distributors were very much on the outer. If you wanted to sell, say Honda and Suzuki, you couldn't stock Yamaha, but Kawasaki was okay. I wasn't too concerned, though I had always considered myself a Yamaha man, I would be sticking with Tom Byrne and the other distributors in the click. Strangely enough, around that time I had an offer from the new Yamaha distributors to join their parts division. A good opportunity as their warehouse was close to home. But again, the loyalty thing again got in the way. They were the enemy; no amount would entice me to change sides.

We rented premises in Bass Hill. John and Mick Pearson had decided to come in with me, though more as silent partners. The shop at Bass Hill was in a far from perfect location being situated in a side street running off the Hume Highway. However, it was all we could afford, and pretty much all that was available at the time.

Before signing the lease, I re-checked with the Honda and Suzuki distributors as to our suitability to be their agents in Bass Hill. Everything was fine they said, all we had to do was open the doors. First lesson in business, get it in in writing. The distributors changed their minds after a dealer in Bankstown convinced them we were too close, and we would go broke. Rubbish of course, well maybe not the go broke part. His business was far from us, the bloke simply didn't want even the slightest whiff of competition. As he was mates with the appropriate sales managers that was that.

So, there we were, the new motorcycle shop in a side street with only Kawasaki. Few people then had even heard of the brand. It would be a battle just to survive.

My first job was a service on a small Honda for a very nice young nurse. I was determined to do the job well, even washing and polishing her machine. When she came to pick it up, she explained she was a little short and asked nicely could she leave her alarm clock as deposit. She would be back soon as she needed the clock to wake in the morning. The bill was $10.00. The clocks value perhaps $1.00. She never returned.

Just as well the Pearson boys were silent partners as we soon discovered the business wouldn't cover even one small wage, let alone three.

As the money ran out, Rosemary volunteered to work nights at local factories. I began to regret ever going into business. We were going backwards and I'd placed a huge burden on the family. Working at nights meant Rosemary missed her girls terribly. I knew if something didn't turn up, and soon, I would have to face reality. Go back to a real job and somehow pay my debts.

The preschool Carol attended was in the charge of a most delightful young woman, as most child care workers are. Carol looked forward to her time there and I always enjoyed seeing the lovely Miss Jane. One Sunday Carol took a fall from her dinky, a nasty crash, though apart from a few scratches and abrasions there was no great damage.

The next morning Carol insisted on going to her Kindy as usual. I dropped her off on my way to work. Miss Jane fussed over Carol telling her how brave she was and Carol trotted off to play with her friends. When I returned in the afternoon all had changed. Jane's usual welcoming smile was replaced with a nasty glare. I felt the venom cut right through me.

Back at G.P. Motorcycles, I asked Carol had she done something naughty. She didn't know what I was talking about and went back to her toys. I let the matter drop thinking perhaps Miss Jane was just having a bad day.

Over the following weeks, nothing changed. No smiles, no welcome, everything was short and sweet. Not a nice feeling when someone you admire and respect so obviously despises you. I began to dread facing Miss Jane. But as far as Carol was concerned the kindergarten was her favourite place. I had little choice but to walk the gauntlet each morning.

A few weeks later, when dropping Carol during the school holidays, Linda was with us. Miss Jane asked if Carol's older sister like to stay the day. Of course she would, anything was better than spending another boring day with her dad at his dead boring motorcycle shop. When I returned in the afternoon all had changed. Miss Jane again smiled. I had been so naïve. Who knew what Miss Jane saw at her kindergarten? I figured she had asked Linda a few discreet questions. I didn't know what sometimes went on behind closed doors. How could I? I learned a lot that year, there really wasn't any Santa Claus.

16
1968

At the end of our first year, and with GP Motorcycles still far from paying its way, the Pearsons decided to pull out of the partnership. I didn't blame them. It wasn't so much they were concerned for their money, more their need to move on. They couldn't see a time when the business would employ the three of us. There were no hard feelings. But ever so slowly the business had been improving. Kawasaki was due to release some exciting new models. I thought perhaps had we had hung on a little longer, we may have made it together. In the end, we decided I would continue on my own and pay them back when the weather broke, or something like that.

I hadn't bothered re-applying for the other franchises. Tom Byrne Pty Ltd was the only distributor who had stuck by me, I was determined to make it as a Kawasaki man.

Another looming problem was my mother. She was about to retire from the railways so her loan would need to be repaid, and soon. The only way I could do that was to close the shop and have a fire sale. I asked Mum if she could give me a little time, and of course Mum did just that. Little did I know help was just around the corner.

One day Gary Innis called into the shop with exciting news. He proudly announced he was a partner in a motorcycle import business. I was gob smacked. Gary and I were close, but this was the first I'd seen of his entrepreneurial side.

Gary, by then was an established sidecar star, he and Carmel ran their own successful butchery at Sydney's upmarket Hunters Hill. Often in the Showground program they referred to Gary as "Sydney's fastest butcher".

Gary and his new partner had somehow secured the NSW agency for the Jawa-C Z range of motorcycles that were manufactured in Czechoslovakia. Included in their lineup was the fantastic ESO (later called Jawa) Speedway Solo machines, ridden or craved by most of the top riders. Gary's partner was heavily into Moto-X sponsorship and was happy to have another dealer market the speedway products. Little did he know there was a huge demand for ESO speedway bikes. Gary knew, but wanted to pass the agency to me, his best friend.

As time went on, Gary became increasingly nervous with his commitment to the business venture as he and Carmel's new house in the northern Sydney suburb of Beacon Hill was on the line.

Eventually Gary decided to pull out of the partnership, but not before I was allocated ten ESO speedway motorcycles, plus a quantity of engines and parts from their first shipment. I couldn't believe my luck, and just when I was about to throw in the towel. By the time the ESOs hit Sydney I had sold the lot. My best friend, the once cheeky young Mascot butcher, had saved my bacon.

Late one Friday afternoon the ESOs were delivered to my shop. Early the next morning a queue of eager customers awaited cash in hand. At days' end, I was unsure what to do with all of the cash as the bank wouldn't open until Monday morning. I decided the safest thing to do was bury the lot in our back yard. My father came out to see what I was up to as I wasn't much of a gardener then. Dad stood stunned when I showed him the bag of money. All his life he had worked his guts out getting nowhere. His much-loved Soldier Settlement Farm hadn't lasted the depression, yet here was his 25-year-old dropout son with a small fortune. We buried the money, and first thing Monday I took it to the safety of the bank. Maybe it wasn't a fortune, but it was a lot of money in the sixties, and the break I so badly needed. By the end of that week I had paid back the Pearsons, and most of all repaid my mother. Gary Innis had saved me; I wouldn't forget that in a hurry.

The arrangement with the Jawa distributor continued and I sold many more new machines, always careful to pay my accounts promptly.

One day, two men in suits called into my shop introducing themselves in heavy European accents. The men were from the Czechoslovak Embassy, and amongst other things informed me there was to be a change in the Jawa-CZ distribution. Before the wall came down all business with Czechoslovakia had to be conducted through their government.

Though the two men were tight lipped, I gathered there had been problems with payment of accounts. I offered to show them check butts covering full payment for all I had received. 'Not necessary,' they said, but I insisted, the last thing I wanted was to have any doubts on my honesty.

Gary Innis had made the right decision to pull out of the business. He still had his house and I still had my business and credit rating. Another lesson learned.

The new distributors were a large retail car company, who for my mind were totally unsuitable to distribute motorcycles. Before long there was another change. In the meantime, I made contact with the South Australian Jawa-CZ distributor and began an association that lasted some years.

Later, on the recommendation of the S.A. distributor, I applied for the NSW agency. In the end the embassy thought me too inexperienced. I guess after their first debacle, they were wary of involvement with another small businessman. Shame really, as I did have the right distribution skills and contacts in the trade. We would have done well together. Maybe I should have tried harder but that's how it goes sometimes.

Then Mum decided she too wanted to have another go in a small business. She had only been retired a short time, but was already well and truly bored. She bought a rundown sandwich shop in of all places, Darlinghurst, or Darlo, as we called the joint. The shop was only a few doors from Sydney's infamous Taylor's Square. Not exactly the place you wanted your mother to spend her days. The square in the late sixties bore little resemblance to today's home of the smart set, more the home of the down and out. A place where they gathered for a sip or two. Many of her customers were ladies of the night from nearby Kings Cross. Didn't worry Mum though, and they got along fine.

Rosemary helped for a while, then Mum employed a pretty young assistant. Susan was a nice kid, and smart, later she established her own secretarial training company at Penrith. I never quite understood why a girl such as Susan came to work in that small Darlinghurst lunch shop. Perhaps it was meant to be, as Susan's father Jack was single, and a good man. Before long he and Mum were an item. They went on to spend many good years together.

My father also met someone that year. Vivian. A lovely lady. So good to see him smiling again.

With Kawasaki sales improving, and the Jawa speedway side of the business at last established. G.P. motorcycles was more than paying its way. To expand I needed to find more suitable premises. Nearby Parramatta was tempting, but as all the major franchises, including Kawasaki, were already accounted for, it was out of the question. I decided to sit tight for the time being, and keep my eyes open.

One afternoon a well-dressed man in his thirties walked into my shop introducing himself as John Galvin. He told me he had just opened a small motorcycle aligned business in nearby Villawood. Uh oh, I thought, this is the bloke I spied on for Tom Byrne. We made the usual small talk. How the industry was going? How was I going, and so on? When I casually mentioned I had previously worked at the BMW distributors he said, 'You've probably heard of me then?' I nodded. He smiled and said, 'It's alright. We've kissed and made up.'

John obviously didn't know of my spying efforts, and as we were getting on so well, I decided not to mention it. When I finally confessed to the spying thing much later, he laughed adding I couldn't have been very good as he was indeed running his own small operation at the time.

There was something about John Galvin I liked. We talked for hours. John explained he had finally made the move from home and taken a lease on a shop in a small shopping centre. I called on him the next morning and soon discovered the reason for his visit. The shop next to his was vacant. John thought if I moved in it would be good for both our businesses. 'Make it sort of a small motorcycle centre,' he reckoned.

His landlord, a Mr. Banovich, owned both premises and was more than happy to make alterations for the small workshop I needed. Over the years, Mr. Banovich would prove the best landlord ever. A good man, an immigrant who had been through the mill.

The people at the local council were a little apprehensive to approve a second motorcycle business in such a small shopping centre. Fortunately, some were speedway fans. Anyway, as it turned out our customers also supported the other businesses and that helped the dying small shopping centre get back its spark.

John Galvin was a motorcyclist's motorcyclist. As a young man he had ridden more miles on the handlebars than most could dream of. John's idea of a motorcycle weekend was to jump on his BMW after work on Friday and ride nonstop till the early hours. It didn't matter if it was winter, or raining, he was in his element. Come Sunday afternoon his dad would have to pry him off the motorbike. Next weekend he'd be off somewhere else. Then he met Margaret, who too was a keen motorcyclist, and highly intelligent. They married and travelled to the U.K. for a working holiday. Once settled in London, John, a television technician by profession, tried his hand at selling motorcycles. Margaret took up a senior position in the newfangled computer world with IBM.

After a couple of good years, homesickness set in and John and Margaret headed for Oz. But there would be no easy flight or ship for the Galvins, they preferred the long way home, beginning with a visit to the Isle of Man T.T. races.

A month or so later, and near the Turkey Iran border, they accepted an offer of sweet tea with a wandering tribesman. Trouble was, according to local custom, John then was required to share the attractive Margaret. A terrible row erupted and police were called. After listening to all sides, they informed Margaret she was expected to watch the poor bloke receive his just punishment in the morning.

In the dead of night, the Galvins packed up and headed into Iran. Then onto Iraq, Pakistan, India and finally Colombo where they loaded the BMW aboard a freighter. After disembarking at Fremantle, they headed across the Nullarbor towards home. Another four thousand kilometers. The road between Eucla and Ceduna then was still dirt, and their R60 BMW no off road bike, but as along with everything else they handled it. Finally, at journey's end, and after some twenty-six thousand miles, even Galvo decided to give touring a miss for a while.

In the Showground Pits

Teddy at home-kid magnet.

Gary Innis (G.I.)

82

17

1969

When Kawasaki released their all new three-cylinder two stroke 500cc rocket ship, they simply called the H1, I began to toy with the idea of making a Speedway comeback on an all new outfit using a H1 engine. The business was ticking over nicely and had grown into one of the state's top Kawasaki dealerships. My competing again on a Kawasaki would be good publicity. But when I mentioned my intention to a few of my sidecar friends they burst out laughing.

'What? Take on the 1000cc Vincents with a 500 two stroke. You're dreaming again Grocott.'

During my "retirement" I had kept my hand in by competing in Moto-X, Trials and Short Circuit events. I simply loved racing motorbikes, and it really didn't matter where or when. I loved the camaraderie with my fellow competitors but deep down I was a Speedway Sidecar Rider, and for me, no other motorcycle competition could take its place.

After a lot of thought, I began work on a 500cc Kawasaki Speedway Sidecar. I didn't have a clue how one would modify a three-cylinder two stroke engine for speedway, so out came my dog-eared copy of Phil Irving's "Tuning for Speed". I figured if I used Phil Irving's tips for tuning single cylinder two stroke moto-x engines it would be a good start. I didn't know what the great man would have thought had he seen me pouring over his book as Aussie Phil Irving was actually the designer of the very bike I was out to beat. The legendary and much loved 1000cc.Vincent V twin.

Since the late forties, Speedway Sidecars and Vincents had fitted each other like a glove. The marque had been almost invincible in Australian sidecar racing, both on speedway and tar. The only motorcycle that had even troubled them during their long reign was the 1000cc V-Twin J.A.P. And here was I about to take them on with an engine half the size.

My ex-passenger Peter White, was then in England learning the ropes and hoping to establish a career in Speedway management and journalism. I wrote to him asking how he felt about a return to the saddle but regretfully he declined. After I retired, Peter had ridden a few meetings with Doug Robson. Following a big one at the Liverpool Raceway, Peter had hung up his leathers for good. In the middle of all this, I had a call from Gary Innis. His regular passenger had decided to cut short an overseas working holiday to return for the summer season. Gary had already lined up Warren Sullivan, a young, experienced and fearless Showground passenger. Not wanting to hurt Warren's feelings, Gary wondered did I know of someone who was looking for a good passenger. I did indeed. Warren Sullivan was a brilliant passenger, and best of all weighed next to nothing, perfect for the lightweight Kawasaki. I rang Warren to explain the situation not sure how he'd react. After all I was certainly no Gary Innis. Warren simply responded with, 'When's our first race?'

After some three years away it sure felt strange to be back in the Showground pits. Fortunately, my old spot next to Doug Robson was vacant, or maybe Doug had kept it that way knowing one day I'd return.

The Kawasaki caused quite a commotion in our first race, the crowd wondering where the howling swarm of bees had come from. We didn't exactly set the world on fire, but Warren and I went home quietly confident that in time the bike would be competitive.

By then Johnny Dunne was an established sidecar rider. He'd pulled some good wins including a Victorian title. Not bad for a new kid and A grade seemed just around the corner. We'd had little to do with each other over the past few years and mixed in different circles. Our once deep and close friendship forgotten to all but a few. John and I had never reconciled, nor had we tried. All too hard. By then John and Carol were parents of a little boy they named of course Teddy. Whenever we passed, we exchanged a polite hello, and kept walking.

Aboard the Kawasaki, my once hard-earned sidecar reputation counted for little. I was again a novice. Even Johnny was giving us a big start in handicap races but to his credit never rubbed it in. Not so the many riders who made us a regular butt of their jokes. All their insults achieved was to make us even more determined.

We finished our first season with a few good wins under our belt and even scored a trip to New Zealand with the NSW team. We knew the N.Z. promoter only wanted us because we were different but it was a good opportunity to gain more experience. We spent a month there. New Zealand riders and mechanics are amongst the best in the world. We returned home with lots of good advice.

Rosemary flew over for the last two weeks of our tour, just in time to see us to crash at Christchurch. There was no great damage, autumn leaves at it again.

Johnny on Teddy's Vincent with passenger Charles Green

18
1970

During the off season we burned much midnight oil. One thing I had learned from that first season, unlike humans, dirt track two stroke engines perform their best on alcohol. We sourced a new set of carburetors from Dell 'Orto in Italy that loved the demon drink. And before the season began, Warren ever the showman, suggested we dye our leathers Kawasaki racing green. I wasn't sure about this as coloured leathers were very out there in 1970. Ninety nine percent of the day's motorcycle racers wore basic black. On the first meeting of the new season, we walked from the change room in our green leathers to a chorus of wolf whistles and catcalls. We were the girly riders on the girly bike, and that suited us just fine.

Some nights in the pits, I'd sneak a glance in Johnny's direction thinking how good would it be if Teddy was still around. The three of us competing at the Sydney Showgrounds like we dreamed all those years before.

Then suddenly things with Johnny began to thaw. One night in the pits he came over and sat on the Kawasaki. We talked small talk. He wished me well in the nights meet, I did the same. Perhaps it wasn't too late to repair our friendship.

Johnny Dunne and I would never reconcile.
Later that night, he was killed in an awful
crash not far from Teddy's place.

The papers had a field day, **"KILLER BIKE CLAIMS SECOND VICTIM", and so on. All the while I couldn't stop thinking of the empty grave next to Teddy. I** so wanted my friends to be together.

After much soul-searching Rosemary called Carol Dunne. Later that week, and before a huge crowd of mourners, Johnny Dunne was laid to rest next to his best friend.

There were phone calls from reporters wanting to do a feature on the three of us. They asked about the grave. Why had I bought it? Did I have a premonition? And so on. I wasn't rude, I simply said it was our story. One I wasn't yet ready to share.

I never considered retirement after Johnny's accident. We had grown so far apart those last years it was almost as if we were strangers. I did grieve for Johnny, but for my old Johnny, I barely knew John Dunne the sidecar racer.

A few weeks after John's funeral, Gordon Guasco called from England. He was coming home for the summer. At last some good news. We talked about the Sydney scene, his daughter Jolie and wife Elaine, and Johnny. In those days before email and twenty-four-hour news, England seemed far away. Though in the tight speedway world, bad news always travelled fast.

Following a successful season in the British Speedway League, Gordon was looking forward to summer with family and friends, and Gordon Gausco had many friends. I was proud to be one.

Gordon, the Fairfield kid with Italian dad and Aussie mum, seemed one who was born to race a motorcycle. Put simply, he could ride like the wind. Talented and artistic, Gordon loved to draw his favourite animals, and again there were many, and always that smile.

Gordon's mum worked behind the bar at the local, and of course everyone in the pub knew young Gordon. He raced with the bicycle skid kids at the old Parramatta speedway. They called him a natural, the kid with the uncanny balance.

Gordon joined the Fairfield Motorcycle Club and began his motorcycle career on the dusty country short circuit tracks. Often he'd have his pet blue tongue tucked safely in his jacket pocket. The fastest lizard in Sydney. Before too long he was B grade, then A grade. Speedway beckoned; his close friend Jimmy Airey was already riding at the Sydney Showgrounds. Gordon was chafing at the bit. They were both Australian Short Circuit champions.

Gordon badly wanted to join Jim but an apprentice sign writer's wage didn't go far. A new bike was needed, but where to raise the money? There was little sponsorship for any sport in the sixties.

The drinkers at the Fairfield Hotel had a weekly lottery thing going. Gordon's mum included him; it was only a few shillings a week. Before long they moved up to the new Opera House Lottery, one hundred thousand pounds first prize. Yes, their number came up. Gordon's share? A cool three thousand, three hundred pounds six and eight pence. More than enough for a new speedway bike.

Gordon's debut at the Kembla Grange track was unlike any other. By season's end, he was starting on the back mark in handicap events. Nothing worried Gordon, he had no fear. If he saw someone he knew on the infield, he'd smile and wave, even in the middle of a full lock slide. Devil may care.

Then it was on to the Sydney Showgrounds, and again much the same story. The Fairfield kid was gifted. Before long he was approached by the U.K. promoters anxious to be the first to sign him. And like so many young hopefuls before him, Gordon made the move to join his Fairfield club mate Jim Airey in the Wolverhampton team. At first Gordon was dreadfully homesick. He missed his family and friends, his lizard, and the other animals. Then Elaine came over and they married in Manchester. Come summer he was back in Oz, now a full-time professional. All around the country he starred in the Aussie test team's many wins. Speedway was Gordon's business by then, and to some it seemed the happy go lucky Fairfield kid was gone forever. But away from the spotlight, he was still the same old Gordon.

Peter White and I had a couple of old Triumphs we sometimes rode at our secret practice track out Botany way. It was just the place where they dumped left over cinders from the old Bunnerong Power Station, but we thought it pretty good. Gordon came along one day, for a while he watched Peter and I go around. Then it was his turn. Gordon didn't care he was wearing his Sunday best. It was the old pre-professional Gordon having the time of his life belting around on a motorbike just for fun. We laughed and we laughed.

A few nights later, Gordon raced in front of thirty thousand fans at the Sydney Showground. No one else saw Gordon ride Botany that day. Peter and I did. And that memory of Gordon Guasco would last us a lifetime. Then he returned to England.

Gordon looked good that Friday as we loaded the new Jawa he was to ride at the Liverpool Raceway. A few years older perhaps, and wiser, but still the same old Gordon. The meeting was washed out and re-run the following Sunday. Another simple accident.

All that long sad week, Gordon's family
and friends held vigil, but it was not to be.
I didn't talk of this with my father.

All these years later, I so regret the lost opportunities. So many things were left unsaid between my father and I. I would have dearly loved to have just sat and talked with Dad. My fault, though I guess the age difference, and war damage, hadn't helped. Dad was seventy-six, I was an immature twenty eight. Different worlds. Different eras. My father had lost much of his spark in the depression years when he was forced to walk away from his much loved farm. I hoped deep down he was a little proud of me. Rosemary was more a daughter than daughter in law and we shared two great kids. Dad had other grandchildren. Jim's three, Gloria's two. But he rarely saw my brother's family who lived in faraway Moree.

Later that year, Dad again left the family home. This time it was a happy occasion. Dad moved to nearby Strathfield, to Vivian, the old soldier content at last. Mum too was on the move. The Darlinghurst sandwich shop was sold and with Jack set off on the big caravanning trip around Australia. I liked and admired Jack, he was a decent man, but deep down I wished it was my father who was driving.

As the speedway season came to an end, we had our best result so far. A close second to Doug Robson in a scratch race. That silenced many of our critics, and there was something they didn't know. Kawasaki were about to release an all-new 750. We were first on the list.

Gordon Guasco
Poole Pirates England

19

1971/1972

GHOSTS IN MY SIDECAR

The new speedway season got underway as we waited patiently for the arrival of our new Kawasaki. By this time Warren worked full time with me at G.P. Motorcycles, we were chafing at the bit to get back out there on the new 750.

As we had been tight lipped about our plans, by our non-appearance, most of the other riders thought we had finally seen the light and ditched the Kawasaki. And quietly hung up those horrid green leathers.

Eventually the big day came, the crate containing our prized motorcycle arrived from Japan. Before removing the engine from the road chassis, I decided to throw on a set of trade plates and take the new bike for a long ride. Rosemary surprised me in asking to come along. She hadn't been on a road motorcycle since our courting days.

Late on Friday afternoon, we set off for Wollongong on the South Coast ridding through the Royal National park and along the southern beaches. On our return I knew the 750 would be a winner. Lots more power at low revs, exactly what was needed for the Showground dirt.

We had taken the chance to nominate for Saturday night and on returning from Wollongong I worked well in the night. By Saturday afternoon all seemed ready, just to be sure we took the bike to the Nepean practice track in far western Sydney for a test ride. It went like a rocket on the small circuit, leaving just enough time to rush home, change, and head for the Sydney Showgrounds.

As we made our way to the start line, I could just hear the track announcer, Steve Raymond, saying we were on an all-new and expensive motorcycle. Then what a letdown. Something was wrong in the fuel department; we ran stone motherless last in every start. Before the end of the meeting we quickly loaded the bike and left with our tails between our legs.

Turned out the problem was minor. The fuel taps, though sufficient for the 500, didn't flow enough methanol for the thirsty 750. Then the long nervous wait until the next Saturday night. All that week Warren and I assured each other everything was right, though silently we weren't completely confident. Even our lowly place on the Showground program was in doubt, as lots of new riders believed they deserved our spot.

The next Saturday night we copped the usual smirks and indifference as we wheeled the 750 through the pit gates and parked next to Doug Robson. Doug looked up and nodded a hello. He asked if everything was sorted. 'Hope so,' was all I could find to say. Doug went back to what he was doing, one of the few who never knocked us. Or perhaps he still felt guilty about the time he sacked me as a passenger. But that was the thing about Doug Robson, he was never the one to criticise a trier.

We warmed up the Kawasaki and waited. I was as nervous as my first race some eight years before, and right back where I started. This time the track announcer had nothing to say as we came to our mark. I guess like everyone else he had given up on us. When the lights went out, I dropped the clutch and the Kawasaki rocketed towards the first turn. So far so good. Next thing we were sideways and accelerated up the back straight faster than I had ever been before, then sideways again into the top corner. I glanced behind at Warren; his right shoulder was rubbing the dirt. My god I thought, we're flying. Half way down the next straight I took a quick look behind, no one, not even close. We went on to win by a mile. Well not quite that, but it was a long way. There were no more fuel problems.

Back in the pits, a crowd gathered to see what we were riding. As the 750 and 500 engines looked much the same, they walked away puzzled.

'What's going on?' someone muttered.

'What's happened to the Kawasaki?' said another. 'Must be using Nitro.'

Same result in the handicap final. The 750 was a rocket ship.

Warren and I went on to win some 28 races in a row. The only downer being the NSW championship when we broke a chain in a semifinal. What a turn around. We were flavour of the month. Reporters called for quotes, everyone wanted to know us. And we were hot favourites for the Australian championships. Who would have believed it?

During the Easter break we travelled to South Australia to compete in the Australian Long Track Championships on the super-fast half mile at Port Pirie. Mum came over to babysit, and I guess hopefully see her youngest son win his first Aussie title. Mum and Jack were regular spectators in Sydney, not so Dad. By then we'd had quite a few writeups in the Sydney newspapers and I hoped perhaps he had read some of them. I saw little of him now that he was living with Vi. When I did, he seemed content.

On first appearance, the track at Port Pirie looked far too rough for our lightweight flyer. Warren and I wondered if it was even worth unloading. One of the local solo riders on seeing the stunned look on our faces walked over. 'Don't worry,' he said. 'That's just the top coat. Helps to keep the moisture in. They'll scrape it off after practice.' He seemed to know what he was talking about so we went out taking it easy. The low-slung Kawasaki bouncing around, even scraping the ground at times.

The large sidecar field was mainly from Victoria and South Australia, and while they had heard of the Kawasaki's Sydney reputation, our efforts in practice hadn't left them too concerned. I overheard someone remark, 'They might have a chance in the 750 class. Not a hope in the big one.'

The track curator did take off the top surface after practice, and the track was good. By the end of the day we had won the 750 and unlimited titles, and set new records in the process.

Back in Sydney we took the kids to the last night of the Royal Easter Show. Usually the show heralded the end of the Showground Speedway season but in 1972, two speedway meetings were to be held after Easter. The first, the Australian Speedway Sidecar Championship.

We sat in the grandstand watching the ring events while Linda and Carol investigated their many show bags. I couldn't take my eyes off the centre ring. In a couple of weeks, it would be again the Showground Speedway. I looked across to where I had stood terrified some twenty years before. So much had changed. The week after the championship I was travelling to Japan with a group of Kawasaki dealers. A long way from a Botany tannery.

April 22nd. 1972.

As Warren and I sat in the pits
nervously awaiting our first race, I felt
John and Ted's presence.

The defending champion was my best friend Gary Innis. In our first heat, we were up against Neil Munro of South Australia, runners up at Port Pirie. The other two riders were from West Australia and Queensland. As the tapes went up, Munro gated fast and led through the first corner and back straight. Then it was all over as we easily sailed past. The track was heavy and wet, Neil and his passenger Rod Lang copped a huge spray from the Kawasaki's back wheel. I glanced behind to see them covered in good old Showground dolomite. The next Monday's edition of the Sydney Sun newspaper had two shots of that moment tagged, "Copped the Lot". One had Neil and Rod covered in dirt, the other Warren and I unmarked.

In the final we gated badly behind Gary and Neil. It's not easy when your soul mate is between you and an Aussie title. I pushed past. Next lap it was Munro's turn, then on to the checkered flag.

We rode slowly to the finish line for the usual prize giving and parade lap. Gary was second, and the first to congratulate us. There weren't any hard feelings, Gary Innis was that kind of man. Rosemary, along with Mum and Jack, called me from the fence. Jack had tears in eyes, it was quite a night. I don't know if my father was there. My sister Gloria and her family were. Perhaps he was, just another face in the crowd.

The next day our phone ran hot with congratulations, and offers from interstate promoters. Quite a change for me. No call from my father, though I hadn't really expected one. He wasn't the kind of man to pick up the phone and make small talk. Nor I. I could have phoned him. I should have. I didn't. If he wasn't at the showground, I hoped at least he would read about it in the paper. I knew I should have taken the time to drive to nearby Strathfield. My excuse? Too busy with business and speedway. My mind on next week's trip to Japan where perhaps there would be some factory recognition for our efforts. In the seventies, Kawasaki were just beginning to make a name for themselves in Australian motorcycle racing. And while speedway wasn't really their thing, it had been very nice free publicity. Speedway then was the only motorcycle sport to receive regular newspaper coverage. Our humble machine had helped introduce the marque to many potential buyers.

Dueling with G.I. and passenger John Lloyd
Sydney Showground 1972

On the outside of Trevor Denman QLD

A kiss from Rosemary

Geoff and Warren
Aussie title night 1972

99

Sinclair Stand Sydney Showgrounds

The week after the Aussie title meet, I left for Japan with a small group of NSW motorcycle dealers. In Tokyo, we met up with the interstate contingent and settled into our five-star hotel. I thought I had died and gone to heaven.

I had a couple of local contacts who had promised to show me around. One was Happy Hirano, a Japanese speed car driver who had toured Australia with some success. The other, Jimmy Ogisu, had done much the same on solos. Happy Hirano, good looking and always well dressed, had a bar on the outskirts of Tokyo. Bob Levy and I were invited to a dinner in our honour at his restaurant. Jimmy would be there, along with a few of the local professional speedway riders.

We seemed to drive for ever as we wound our way through the narrow back streets of Tokyo and not once did I see a single foreigner. I was a long way from downtown Botany.

Later we moved onto the speedway circuit. So different. More like the horse racing with betting & bookmakers. Jimmy and Happy took us through the pits introducing us around. I had no idea what he was saying, though the riders seemed friendly enough. They were full time professionals, much like our jockeys. And the thing I liked best; no animals were hurt during the racing. No humans either as it turned out. Jimmy asked if I wanted to place a bet, and of course my pick ran last. Who cared, it was a great night.

We visited the Kawasaki plant where I was informed I would be presented with a new engine courtesy of the factory. I had never chased sponsorship, preferring to be independent, anyway there weren't many sponsors around in the early seventies. Speedway riders were at least paid start and prize money, and when you compared this with other sportspeople of the era we didn't do too badly. Once I switched to the modern and reliable Kawasaki, I began to make a profit from competing. Different story with the Vincent, where the constant replacing of old expensive parts left little in the kitty.

As we wandered around the plant, I had a long conversation with the West Australian distributor George Cowie who was there with his son Kevin. A few months before, Mum and Jack had written from the west singing its praises. I was keen to know more about the place. George too, had been a sidecar racer in his youth, while Kevin was currently an A grade road racer. We got on well and later, in the way of West Aussies, George said, 'If you ever want to come across to God's country, give me a call. I can always use a good man.'

Back at home, the new engine arrived as promised but I left it untouched for the time being and got back into work and normal life. In the meantime, Warren decided to return to his trade accepting a position of maintenance carpenter at Sydney University. I reluctantly said goodbye. We had been through a lot, though for some reason I had a feeling our days were numbered. Warren was a very good motorcycle rider in his own right, and had his own ambitions. The one thing that had kept us focused was our determination to prove we could win the Aussie title on something different.

After Warren left, I employed a local lad, Reggie Wright. He was young and keen, and willing to learn. We made a good team.

Warren got hitched that winter. I was best man. He had been married before, though both were very young at the time. After a while they parted with no hard feelings. There was a son, Colin.

The wedding was a flash affair at a reception centre in Bexley. Just around the corner from the house I moved to with Mum after my parent's break up. The venue was directly opposite the bus stop where I had often waited when commuting to T-Shoes in Botany. Unpleasant memories.

Deep down I had a feeling Warren's marriage would go the way of my parents. I just couldn't see this was the right move for him.

20
1972/3

Once more spring came around and we were back to Saturday nights at the Showground Speedway. Much had changed. Being the reigning Australian champions meant we would be starting from the back mark in handicap races. Hard going, starting 120 yards behind the front markers in a three-lap race. Privately, I questioned the wisdom of my continuing to ride speedway. Every time I raced, I felt Johnny and Ted's ghosts telling me to stop. Somehow, I knew if I didn't, sooner or later I would join them. With the thrill of the chase over, I preferred to be home with my family. Still, every Saturday night I loaded the Kawasaki for the long nervous drive to the city. Rosemary felt the same, though she hadn't interfered hoping I would make the decision on my own. I knew I was pushing my luck, but our business and friends were tied up with speedway. It had been my life for some thirteen years; it would be hard to make the break.

And Warren's new marriage wasn't going at all well. He was under lots of personal pressure and for the first time we began to argue. He thought my riding off, and he was probably right. Slowly but surely our once close partnership began to fall apart.

One night after a lousy showing we decided to call it quits. Just like that. I watched as he walked out the pit gate carrying the green leathers we had once taken so much pride in wearing. It was over.

21

1973

SYDNEY to PERTH

After Warren left, I asked my old business partner John Pearson if he'd like to ride a few meets to see how we'd go. John hadn't ridden passenger for some time as he and Brother Mick had sold their Vincent after Mick suffered serious back injuries in a road accident. Also, I was sure the accident with Teddy had long weighed on his mind. We ordered another pair of green leathers.

Turned out it wasn't a good move for John, as we only rode a few meetings before a big one. John wasn't Warren, I hadn't allowed for that.

I awoke in the ambulance, while John in the main was unhurt. I had been very lucky as part of my vertebrae was crushed.

The next morning I was allowed to leave St. Vincent's hospital, on the proviso I would see my own doctor for further treatment.

After a few weeks' physiotherapy, I thought I was again ready to ride and of course against the advice of my doctor.

First meeting back, we again crashed being unable to avoid a sidecar team who had spun in front of us. Luckily, we were unhurt, the other rider, Graham Young, suffered a broken leg. Again, my bike was a wreck and this time I decided to give it a rest for a while.

Back to physio three times a week, I was exhausted and having trouble staying awake during the sessions. After a few weeks, the physiotherapist said, 'Mate, you need a holiday.' I explained it was out of the question, I had a business to run. 'Well at least take a few days off to look at your options. And bloody well rest.'

Reluctantly I took her advice and we headed to the Central Coast for a short break in a waterfront hotel. Young Reg was left in charge of the shop. Big responsibility, but John Galvin was next door if needed.

The short holiday did wonders. The kids swam and ate, ate and swam, while I slept. At night after our exhausted daughters were in bed Rosemary and I sat on the hotel front lawn and talked. I was about to turn thirty-one, and while motorbikes in the main been good to us, I didn't know how long it would take for my spark to return, if ever. Perhaps it was time for a change. Rosemary had read an advertisement for new houses in Perth. Real estate then was cheap in the west. If we sold the house and business, we would have more than enough for a small acreage. Maybe it was time to give the self-employment thing a miss and take a job with the Perth Kawasaki distributors I'd met in Japan.

Back at GP Motorcycles young Reg and I battled on. He did all the heavy workshop work while I stayed in the showroom. We were still doing well, selling lots of new Kawasakis, and the odd speedway bike. The Aussie dollar was strong against the Japanese yen, small motorbikes inexpensive. Apart from Jawa speedway bikes, we sold only Kawasaki. Because of this we were one of the biggest volume Kawasaki dealers in NSW. All from our small shop in a side street at suburban Villawood.

Then came the call from Mr. Whyte at Tom Byrne Pty. Ltd. They had lost the Kawasaki distributorship.

First Yamaha, then Kawasaki. After all Tom Byrne's missionary work the agency was being handed to a large public car company. Obviously, the factory thought they would do a better job. Would have been nice had they first consulted some of their dedicated dealers. I wasn't sure I wanted to have anything to do with the new company. Mr. Whyte advised me to wait and not do anything drastic. As always, my mentor was the voice of reason. I took his advice.

I soon learned the new distributors were a large public company trading as LNC Industries. They had lots of fingers in the pie, amongst other things, the Australian distributorship for Volkswagen, then a big player in the Australian car market. They also distributed Jeep and Audi, and had recently introduced Subaru from Japan. Apparently one of their branches in Queensland had acquired that state's Yamaha distributorship as part of a takeover deal hence their new interest in motorcycles. Many businesses could see potential in the fast-growing motorcycle industry and were looking for a piece of the action. I wasn't impressed with any of this, for me they were simply Carpetbaggers.

At that time, there was a good quid to be made in motorbikes. The new Kawasaki Z1 900 cc had a large dealers commission, and as the model was in short supply there was no need to discount. What a time for Tom Byrne Pty. Ltd. to lose the agency.

We dealers were invited to a getting to know you meeting at LNC's head office in North Sydney. Most of the NSW Kawasaki dealers turned up anxious to see what changes were in the air. From the time I parked the car and walked to their building I was in a world far removed from the small city shopfront of Tom Byrne Pty. Ltd. The LNC headquarters sat high in a modern building in Sydney's prosperous north. A spectacular glass elevator ran on the outside. Never one fond of heights I opted for the inside lift and made my way to the conference room.

After a little softening we listened to the usual blurb, 'We're going to do this for you. We're going to do that for you. Blah blah blah.'

I really didn't want to be there. I was still recovering from my injuries, and I've always had an aversion to bullshit. I thought to myself, 'Who are you to tell me what you're going to do with Kawasaki. What have you ever done for motorcycles?'

In their immaculate suits, the new general manager and sales manager gave a slick presentation, though I doubted they'd ever been on a motorcycle. Turned out I was wrong as far as the sales manager went. He was a motorcyclist, a road racer in the UK. He at least had ridden the odd bike, and had a little industry experience, albeit over there. The general manager was very much the young man going places from their car side of

106

things, and expected to do big things with the new agency. While they spruiked, I was fighting to stay awake, a usual occurrence since the accident. I buried my head in my hands hoping no one would notice my sleepy eyes. I could never imagine myself out there dressed in a suit giving a sales talk. With Mr. Whyte, everything was low key. No crap, just how I liked it.

The new mob hammered home how they were a progressive company with the latest technology, including the first computer in the auto parts industry. We were invited to see the new one-million-dollar technical whiz thing in its air-conditioned home at their parts department in nearby North Ryde. They pointed out we would have printouts of parts prices, and so on. Things that weren't even imagined in the early seventies. Everything then was done manually, there was no such thing as print outs of stock levels and prices. When they told us this new thingo they called a computer even did away with the need for stock cards, I wondered what would happen to the record clerks at Leyland Motors. I walked away from the meeting with the vision of men in suits telling me how to sell motorbikes. This new mob wasn't for me.

Fast forward to Perth 1974

Another man in a suit is telling Kawasaki dealers how to sell motorcycles. The man in the suit is me. I had joined the enemy.

22

1973

PERTH-WESTERN AUSTRALIA

There are two Perths in Australia. One is a beautiful small historic town not far from Launceston Tasmania. Being the Gypsy I am, I would almost end up there many years later. There was this beautiful historic stone house by the Esk River for sale. Perfect for a B&B. Like many of my dreams, it was never to happen.

On a whim, we sold G.P. Motorcycles and hit the road first stopping in Adelaide to defend the Aussie title. Of course, I went rotten, I just wanted to get the night over and leave in one piece.

A couple of days later, and half way along the rough dirt section of the Nullarbor, our trailer's axle let go. It wasn't repairable. We had money coming, but it was some time away. Plus, I had just learned the position I'd lined up in Perth was no longer. Seemed the mob who had taken over Kawasaki in Sydney, had done the same thing in the west. We were stranded at Ivy Tanks, half way along the dusty and rough Nullarbor Plain.

The bloke who ran the Ivy said we could have his trailer, for a price. Fortunately, he was a speedway fan and went easy. Even offered me a job running the place. Six weeks on-six weeks off. The girls would do their school stuff by radio. Rosemary would run the motel. Sounded good to me. Ivy Tanks was just an old service station, motel and car graveyard soon to be bypassed by the new road. Because of that, the place was a bit run down. Though in the middle of the Nullarbor, beggars couldn't be choosers.

108

Rosemary sort of agreed it might be a bit of adventure, until she saw all the dead critters in jars the bloke's wife had collected around the place. Half an hour later we were back on the Nullarbor.

We survived the first couple of months in Perth by selling Rosemary's much-loved Lotus Ford Escort, replacing it with "BERTHA", a well-worn white Valiant wagon. Rosemary took a job as a sandwich hand while I took to being a spare parts counter jumper again. When the call from the enemy came, all my principles and loyalty were quietly put aside.

Late one afternoon I was ushered into the Managing Director's office at Western Motor Company, a division of LNC Industries in Sydney, aka the enemy. The Managing Director, a Mr. Gartrell, waved his hand, 'Take a seat Geoffrey. Nice to finally meet you.'

'Nice to meet you, Mr. Gartrell.'

'Call me Bruce old boy. Can I get you something?'

I mentioned a cup of tea and my new best friend picked up the phone. A few minutes later his secretary appeared tea in hand, and bikkies.

I couldn't work out who looked the best, Bruce or his huge office. Both were immaculate. I felt out of place, uncomfortable, though thankfully Rosemary had dressed me for the occasion. With a nice business shirt and tie, at least I looked the part. Rosemary did an inspection before I left saying, 'Try not to spill anything on it!'

Good idea my wearing long sleeves, they covered the tat on my right forearm. The one with Pam in the middle. The one I promised Rosemary I would have covered with flowers one day.

Mr. Gartrell talked a little small talk while I was trying hard not to sound like a Botany Boy. Mr. Gartrell too was from Sydney; the motorcycle thing was a complete unknown for him. After a while he said, 'Well Geoffrey, would you like to come on board?'

On board? I wasn't exactly sure what that entailed, but after all the drama of the past months it sure sounded good.

'What did you have in mind Bruce?'

'Head Kawasaki W.A. Set the thing up. Make it happen.'

I gulped.

'You'll start as State Sales Manager. All goes well, General Manager.'

Gulped again.

109

'There'll be the usual company car, expense account and so on.'

I could only manage a nod.

'We'll sort something with a salary. Of course, it will be up for review.'

And that was that. I was to be an executive.

As I walked from the Managing Director's office, I felt the many office staff's eyes on me. I had this strange urge to roll up my sleeves, show them my tats, and yell loudly, 'Fancy you lot hiring a scrubber from Botany.' Of course I didn't and just kept walking with a smile on my face. It reminded me of the old rock song where the bloke reads the help wanted sign that says, "No long-haired freaky people need apply." He tucks his hair under his cap, walks in and gets the job. That done, he whips off the cap and yells, 'Imagine that, me working for you.' There was a message there somewhere but I didn't yell. I knew Rosemary would be proud of me and after the Lotus Escort car thing, and all the other crappy stuff, she needed something positive.

LNC knew what they were doing. They'd done their homework. The West is far from NSW, and the previous distributors, the Cowie family, were, like Tom Byrne Pty. Ltd. in Sydney, highly regarded. LNC knew local dealers would not be impressed with some eastern states company muscling in on their motorcycle trade. So, who better to represent them than one who'd seen the light and moved west? And he spoke their language.

One day not long after taking up my position, I looked on as a consignment of spare parts and motorcycles arrived from our Sydney office. On the side of one of the boxes someone had written in large letters, **"UP BOTANY"**. I stopped and stared, for too long it seemed as a storeman came over and asked if I was alright. I nodded and walked off. He had probably never heard of Botany, and I sure wasn't about to tell him of my humble beginnings. But for a long time after, I wondered just who at our Sydney branch knew I was a Botany boy, and no suit and tie would ever change that.

A few weeks later when I was in Sydney being indoctrinated, I waited for some Botany person to introduce him or herself. Never happened and their identity remained a mystery to me.

While in Sydney I called on my father at the apartment he shared with Vivian. Actually, it was her apartment as Dad had given most of his money to us three children. Material possessions were never his thing. Though he had worked hard and was thrifty, for him there was more to life than accumulating personal wealth or trinkets. Perhaps another legacy of his years in WW1.

That day he was relaxed and happy. It was obvious they were very much in love. Vivian's family had welcomed him to the fold, and finally my father was at peace. For a long time, we sat and talked.

Dad seemed proud with my new station in life. I invited them to visit as soon we bought a home in the west. Everything was well between us.

As I left, I noticed a small framed press cutting on the sideboard. My father was proud of me.

It was the last time I would see my father. On September 13th. 1973, Dad passed away in Concord Repatriation Hospital. It was sudden, and I wasn't there. So many things were left unsaid, and just when I was beginning to grow up.

Forward to another time and another place. It's 1998, and I'm old. Perhaps not old, but older. I'm driving a night cab in Sydney on a hot Saturday night.

Around nine, two blokes in their early thirties jump in the back. They're off to the Surf Rock, a sort of nightclub and bar at Collaroy on the northern beaches.

We're cruising along Pittwater Road and the song, "In the living Years" comes on the radio. Suddenly all is quiet. In the

rear-view mirror I see one of the blokes
crying.

Outside the Surf Rock his mate pays the
fare and whispers, 'He's just lost his dad.'

Drive on.

The Sydney house sold a few weeks later and helped lift me from my depression. Our house hunting was on in earnest. One property in the Perth Hills had taken our fancy, a nice house on six acres backing onto state forest. Come the open day, along with other hopefuls, we were sitting on the front verandah, and dreaming. We looked down to the lush citrus orchard that filled the bottom acre and slowly fell in love.

The homestead, built in the traditional Australian farm design, had a wood stove in the kitchen and a large fire place in the lounge overlooking the front garden. The vendors, two women, had it built to their plans some ten years before. They knew their stuff. They were both nursing sisters returning to the NSW central coast for a well-earned retirement. And there we were, also from NSW, hoping to be the next owners. All this I learned from the agent as the shy women were nowhere to be seen.

At the rear of the home was a very well-built chicken run and shedding, and next to that a small commercial strawberry plot. I had never so much as grown a tomato, but I knew we would be happy here. The back few acres were natural bush that flowed into the state forest.

Our hopes were dashed when the agent informed us the reserve would be in the order of forty thousand dollars. As our limit was thirty-two we left disappointed.

The following Saturday we were back on the hunt. This time our attention was focused on a stone house with three acres on the same road as the dream property. The stone house had been advertised that morning with an asking price of thirty-two thousand. We hoped to negotiate it down to thirty, well within our budget.

We called at the agent to arrange an inspection but the office girl couldn't help. Seemed everyone was attending an auction in Phillips Road. Of course, at the house we'd fallen in love with. We had decided not to attend the auction as we couldn't face seeing some lucky person walk off with our dream home.

I explained to the assistant we had driven up from Perth to see the house they advertised. 'Sorry about that,' she said. 'If you like, you can go and have a look, the vendor's son should be there.' I asked would she contact the salesman and have him meet us but it all seemed too hard.

We drove on to the stone house, and the son indeed was home, but she had forgotten to say he was about eight years old, and with no idea what was going on. Still, after looking around, we thought if the price was right it would do.

When we had finally finished nosing around, and boring the eight-year-old with dumb questions, it was time for lunch. Suddenly Rosemary announced she had changed her mind and wanted to attend the auction. 'Don't forget Geoffrey, the buyers will be our neighbours.'

We arrived just as the proceedings were about to get under way, with the auctioneer holding centre stage on the front lawn. How many of the large crowd were buyers or tyre kickers like us, I didn't know. It was the first auction we had been to, and very exciting. The girls took off to who knew where while we tried to blend in.

From the picture in his office I recognised the absentee opposition salesman leaning against the fence. He appeared to be quite content just watching the proceedings. Little did he know there was every chance he too would make a big sale that day. Were he in his office, we would have in all probability been signing an agreement to purchase the stone house there and then.

Right on time the bidding started, and with a vengeance. Too fast for me to follow. Suddenly it stalled at thirty-four thousand and for some unknown reason I called out, 'Thirty-five!' Rosemary gasped and whispered, 'What are you doing?' I whispered back 'Don't worry, it won't stop there.' It did.

Next thing, the auctioneer was saying something like, 'I will have to speak with the vendors.' And all eyes were focused on the seemingly wealthy

113

young couple who had made the final bid.

Perhaps the other prospective buyers thought we were just getting warmed up and so pulled out of the race. Little did they know it was our first and final bid, and already way over our budget. Thirty-five thousand was a lot of money in Perth in 1973, a lot of money anywhere.

After what seemed a long wait the agent returned smiling, 'Congratulations. You've bought yourself a fine property.'

The crowd applauded and slowly shuffled off. Rosemary was shell shocked. Me too. Our girls thought it great.

We went inside to meet the vendors who had hidden when the bidding commenced. They wanted to meet the people who so obviously loved their home.

The vendors poured themselves a large scotch, and another for Rosemary who was still shaking. I was a little shaky as well as I had to write a cheque for ten percent of the purchase price. Trouble was we only had seventy bucks in our account. Oh well, we had a few days up our sleeve before it would hit the bank.

I rang Mum to tell her the news, and ask if she knew where the proceeds of the house sale were. Mum reminded me it was a long weekend in Sydney but not so in Perth, meaning we were down a day.

After a nervous wait all ended well and the house at Mundaring was ours, and the banks, though that wouldn't be for a while as we had a three months' settlement.

We held the usual house warming inviting all our new Perth friends. Our buying the house had made us sort of honorary West Aussies. We were accepted in the fold.

The girls enrolled at the local primary school and a few weeks later Rosemary applied for the position of secretary to the headmaster and was successful. At last things were going swimmingly.

For the first few weeks I just wanted to walk around our six acres and sit on the front verandah in the twilight. I had a lot to learn about gardens and orchards, but this beautiful green paradise was ours, and life couldn't get much better. I didn't know then about Perth summers.

The speedway season at Claremont was already underway, and still hesitant about my competing, I discussed the matter with my boss Bruce Gartrell. He felt, while in general LNC Industries frowned on their executives competing in motorsport, he was sure they'd make an exception for their new motorcycle people. Apparently, a few of the LNC bigwigs had seen me ride at the Sydney Showgrounds and were quite pleased I had joined the company. It was up to me. A few weeks later I rang the Claremont promoter to nominate for the following Friday evening.

Perhaps I'd been spoiled by competing at the superb and professionally run Sydney Showgrounds. No matter how hard I tried to like Claremont Speedway, for me it just didn't have the same class. Not that the West Aussies didn't love their speedway turning up in their many thousands while the announcer constantly informed them Claremont was the greatest speedway in Australia, if not the world. On a per capita basis Perthites attended speedway in greater numbers than anywhere else in Australia, and its competitors were rewarded handsomely, perhaps it was the best.

At some 640 yards around Claremont was a long and wide track, much safer than Sydney's narrow banked 550 yards. It should have suited the Kawasaki, but it was rough, very rough, due in the main to the running of car and bike events concurrently.

I had an ordinary first night. My new passenger Tony Ecclestone, though an experienced road race passenger, found the going hard. He wasn't alone. We were wearing my lucky GP Motorcycle's body colours, the same ones I had used on many tracks in the eastern states and New Zealand. They didn't last one night at Claremont, ripped to threads. I wasn't impressed.

In the change room after the meeting, one of the local passengers asked what I thought of their track, 'Ridden on better paddocks.' was all I could find to say. West Aussies don't appreciate men from the east knocking their stuff and he terminated our conversation abruptly. His name was Ray Barbour, a likeable young bloke who rode for Dennis Nash, one of the state's two top riders. The other sidecar star was Graham Harris who had competed in Sydney the night I won the Aussie. Dennis Nash would go on to win five Australian Championships. There was little love lost between the two Claremont sidecar heavyweights, seemed to me they'd go to any length to beat each other, it was personal. I watched them from close behind in a scratch race, all the while thinking to myself, these two are off the air. I gave them a wide berth, but that's no way to win races.

The next meeting, we improved a little, but when we arrived the following week, we had been dropped to the encourage race. An insult. The promoter

115

apologised assuring me it was a printing error. I didn't believe him. From our first meeting, I had never taken to the man. He reminded me of a carnival spruiker and I figured this was his way of putting me in my place.

With my back well and truly up we got on with the nights racing. By meetings end we had won all our starts, including the scratch. I loaded the Kawasaki and drove home to Mundaring. And that was that.

What can I say about my speedway days?
I lost good friends, made others that would last a lifetime. Perhaps I'd only been a one hit wonder but thankfully, apart from a few broken bones and a crushed vertebra, I had survived pretty much intact. If not for speedway and motorbikes I may have well stayed in the tannery.

Two weeks later, Ray Barbour was killed in an awful accident at Claremont. I felt partly responsible as I saw it coming. Should I have warned him? Would he have listened? I doubt it.

All these years later I remember Ray, and the others, but especially Teddy Preston and Johnny Dunne.

The Sydney Showground Speedway
1926 – 1996

In memory of the speedway riders and drivers who lost their lives competing at the Sydney Showground Speedway (The Royale) which once ringed this site. They started their last race here, at the Start/Finish line, but were never greeted with the chequered flag.

This plaque, dedicated this day 10.11.2000 by Mr Jim Shepherd on behalf of:

The Veteran Speedway Riders Association of Australia
NSW Vintage Compact Speedcar Club
The Vintage Speedcar Association (NSW) Inc
The NSW Vintage Modified Association
And the many loyal fans

Name	Class	Date
James Donaghy	Solo	26.02.1927
Frank Harris	Solo	06.12.1930
Bert Brennan	Solo	03.12.1932
Freddie Paul	Solo	03.12.1932
Frank Elms	Solo	21.12.1935
Jack Skelton	Sidecar	04.01.1947
Norm Hardy	Sidecar	12.04.1947
Kev Gallaher	Speedcar	07.10.1949
Jim Hansbury	Solo	07.03.1953
Brian Moles	Speedcar	03.11.1956
Bob Staples	Solo	15.12.1956
Merv Dowling	Sidecar/Pass.	09.03.1957
Sam Stanton	Speedcar	24.01.1959
Peter Johnson	Speedcar	07.01.1961
Jack Bissaker	Speedcar	21.10.1961
Barry Robinson	Speedcar	30.11.1963
Nick Collier	Speedcar	27.02.1965
Barry Hopkin	Solo	13.11.1965
Ted Preston	Sidecar	05.02.1966
Denis Duggan	Sidecar/Pass.	29.10.1966
Lionel Levy	Solo	10.02.1968
Ken Mapp	Solo	28.09.1968
Roger Browne	Solo	15.02.1969
John Dunne	Sidecar	24.10.1970
Geoff Curtis	Solo	15.12.1973

Hollywood's take on Australian Sidecar racing
Speedway scenes were shot at Sydney Showground.

Made in the USA
Coppell, TX
26 September 2021

62902664R00070